We Are What We Ate

We Are What We Ate

24 MEMORIES OF FOOD

edited by

MARK WINEGARDNER

A Harvest Original • Harcourt, Inc.

Orlando Austin New York San Diego Toronto London

Library of Congress Cataloging-in-Publication Data
We are what we ate/edited by Mark Winegardner.
p. cm.
"A Harvest original."
ISBN 0-15-600623-5
1. Gastronomy. 2. Food. 3. Food Habits—United States.
I. Winegardner, Mark, 1961-.
TX631.W38 1998
641'.01'3—dc21 98-18032

Designed by Lydia D'moch
Printed in the United States of America
B D F H J K I G E C

Permissions acknowledgements appear on p. vi,
which constitutes a continuation of the copyright page.

All contributors to *We Are What We Ate* have generously donated their work to Share Our Strength.

Share Our Strength works to alleviate and prevent hunger and poverty in the United States and around the world. By supporting food assistance, treating malnutrition and other consequences of hunger, and promoting economic independence among people in need, Share Our Strength meets immediate demands for food while investing in long-term solutions to hunger and poverty. To meet its goals, Share Our Strength mobilizes industries and individuals to contribute their talents to its antihunger efforts and creates community wealth to promote lasting change.

Share Our Strength
1511 K Street, NW, 940
Washington, DC 20005

Contents

Introduction
Mark Winegardner
1

Picky Eater
Julia Alvarez
18

Onion Pie
Paul Auster
32

My Son, Eating Dinner
Charles Baxter
38

Manje
Madison Smartt Bell
46

The Pleasures of Eating
Wendell Berry
54

We Eat the Earth
Janet Burroway
66

Watercress
Elena Castedo
75

Nothing to Eat but Food:
Menu as Memoir
John Dufresne
80

Spaghetti
Robert Girardi
93

In a Leaf of Collard, Green
Jessica B. Harris
105

Chinese Spareribs
David Haynes
110

Don't Ask, Just Eat
Gish Jen
123

Entrée Nous
Beverly Lowry
126

The Burden of the Feast
Bobbie Ann Mason
135

Her Chee-to Heart
Jill McCorkle
146

The Famine of Bengal
Gita Mehta
156

Eat Your Pets
Ellen Meloy
158

Chop Suey Xmas
Lorrie Moore
168

Bitter Honey Cake
Josip Novakovich
173

Brain Food
Chris Offutt
180

Tots
Stewart O'Nan
184

Pork
Richard Russo
191

Lady Food
Lee Smith
201

Grandma's Table
Steve Yarbrough
205

Afterword
William H. Shore
221

List of Contributors
224

Introduction

I grew up in a two-story brick house that never had an onion in it.

(I'm exaggerating. First of all, two other families lived in that house before we did, and I can't speak to their attitudes vis-à-vis the pungent onion. Also, I didn't live in that house until I was seven. Before that, I lived in a double-wide house *trailer,* on the edge of town. A small cornfield separated us from the trailer court my grandfather owned, operated, and sold most of the trailers into. We bought corn at the store anyway, usually in cans. Why we didn't just swipe it from that field—which, after all, belonged to my grandfather—is one of the mysteries of my

childhood. Another one is why my mother, now staunchly liberal, voted for Richard Nixon three times. I'm also unclear about [a] why, when we did move into a real house, that brick one in town, we gave away my dog Scamp; [b] what I was so hacked off about that made me fight so much with my little sister Shari; and [c] why my father never kept beer in the house.)

I grew up during the 1970s, coming of age in Gerald Ford's postgroovy America, in a small town in northwesternmost Ohio, in a house that never had a clove of garlic in it. Our house never contained any spices other than salt (crystalline NaCl, not technically a spice), pepper (even a blind chicken finds the rare kernel of peppercorn), sugar (a water-soluble crystalline carbohydrate, not technically a spice), and the dull, sweet brown ones my mother used for a few days each fall, to bake apple and pumpkin pies. In my house, curry would have been more exotic than heroin.

(Again I'm invoking a fraudulently obtained poetic license. Fact is, the spices were kept in the liquor cabinet, which was built into the pantry: two shelves high, two feet wide, and lockable. It contained rarely employed containers of garlic powder, vodka, rum, onion powder, crème de menthe, and this one tiny, forlorn tin of stale Kroger's-brand chili powder, which survived the entirety of my childhood. My father drank, but not the booze. Warm, incomplete fifteen-packs of Stroh's, purchased because it

came with three extra cans for the same price as most twelve-packs, were hidden in the garage, basement, and under mossy logs in the woodpile out back. My father neither ate nor drank for taste. My mother did; she liked the limey haze of vodka gimlets, but had maybe five a year. The most threatening thing in that liquor cabinet was the chili powder. On those giddy occasions someone had an impulse to add a pinch of it to some bland meat-based thing simmering bleakly atop the avocado green range, my mother would say, "Careful, careful!" After I got out of college I helped my parents move to a house in a town eighteen miles south of there. The town was called Defiance. Still is. The trailer dealership that my grandfather had started in the 1930s, and that my parents had bought from him in the early '70s and presided over during the lingering bankruptcy of, was called Winegardner Mobile Homes. Was. My mother, who'd taught herself bookkeeping so she could keep that cost in-family, saved her and my father's bacon by landing a cost-accounting job at a big factory in Defiance. My father became an insurance agent, although, broken by the failure of the business his father had started, he spent almost every day driving to Fort Wayne and going to the movies, having an affair with Twizzlers, vats of popcorn, and whatever Hollywood sent to the Southtown Mall Cineplex, rather than with another woman, like a normal father would have. The day I packed

up my parents' kitchen, that thing of chili powder was still there. There was about a quarter of it left. The Kroger's where it was purchased had gone bankrupt—fourteen years earlier than Winegardner Mobile Homes.)

Here's what meals were like in the spiceless, unseasoned house of my youth. My parents would come home from work. Typically this would mean my mother emerging haggard from the back-bedroom home office, tired and drawn from the hopeless state of the trailer sales' finances, and my father returning home from the sales lot in an oil-dripping, company-owned Chevy Suburban. Sometimes, though, my mother would be at the lot, too; sometimes my father snuck out of work and spent the afternoon with his metal detector, digging up pop tabs in a park someplace. Wherever. They would meet in the kitchen. One of them would unwrap the pound of hamburger that had been thawing all day in the sink. Stove on. Teflon skillet out (a lighter shade of avocado green than the range top).

Plop the meat in the skillet. Remove the Styrofoam thing.

Brown the meat.

Then, and only then, figure out what's going to go in it.

One favorite: a family-sized can of baked beans, augmented with a cup of ketchup (not a vegetable) and a half-cup of brown sugar (not a spice). Stir well. Serve hot.

That was one of the good ones. Often, if a "recipe" failed to occur to them, they would pour in a can of

tomato sauce (the kind with other stuff in it, including spices, hadn't yet been invented) and keep thinking.

Some of the things they decided to put with it might, in these more enlightened times, constitute child abuse. On more than one occasion they stirred in a bagful of frozen vegetables. Peas. Peas and carrots. Corn. Lima beans.

This would be served up with no apology, on harvest-gold–trimmed Corelle dinner plates, ladled so full the trim was submerged.

"What is it?" I would often say.

"Chili," my mother would say. "Eat it."

My mother and father would discuss their doomed efforts to keep their mom-and-pop small-town trailer sales afloat.

"He made a face at me!" my sister would say.

"I did not," I'd say, and kick her under the table.

"Ow!" she'd say. If they had not been watching us, she'd claim that I'd hit her in the eye, which always got me in more trouble, typically a spanking with the fraternity paddle my father had gotten at Ohio University before he dropped out.

"He hit me in the eye!" she'd say.

"Are you going to eat that?" my father would say after I'd been spanked.

"Yes," I'd say. Terrible food, and the helpings too small.

(I'm not being fair. First of all, by the standards of the

place and time I grew up, my parents' "cooking" wasn't so different than my friends' parents'. Second, if I'm honest—which, let's face it, we can never be, with the past; truth is a parenthetical component of memory—I don't remember thinking at the time about how horrible the food was. This reflects badly on me, not them, and, to compensate, I have spent my adult life eating as much spicy and/or exquisite food as I can. Third, *nothing* my parents could have done would have saved that business; *all* small-town mom-and-pop trailer sales went bankrupt in the '70s, flushed to oblivion alongside the eight-track tape and unironic patriotism. Fourth, as I cannot stress enough, my mother baked fine pies. Still does. Fifth, when my father finally joined AA, which in fact happened four years before his business went broke, I was surprised; I do not have a single true memory of him being drunk. Finally, I have created the impression that chili-free "chili" was all we ever ate. It wasn't. To vary our menus they also performed analogous feats on boxed Kraft mac'n'cheese and called those "casseroles." Try it. Important stir-ins include peas, tuna fish, undiluted cans of either Campbell's tomato or Campbell's cream of mushroom soup, or some unholy combination thereof. Dinners that did not feature "chili" or "casseroles": tartare-centered, burned-crisp hamburgers or steak, gas-grilled while my father inspected the woodpile; dishes involving Miracle Whip; Raisin Bran; instant mashed potatoes baked over a layer of canned corn

and a layer of browned meat; oven-burned steroid-fed
chicken, treated with preservative-laden Shake 'n Bake
[and I helped]. Plus, there was always room for Jell-O.
While I am plumbing lies for truth, I should also say that
my father, sober and thus sans the attractive nuisance of
warm beer in the woodpile, continued to burn all grilled
meat to ash. Still does.)

God bless the miraculous advent of Hamburger
Helper: boxed, salty, noodley, cheesy, the same every time.
Hamburger Helper/Helps your hamburger, went the prod-
uct's TV jingle, *Help you/Make a great meal.*

Help had arrived. We tried every variety the super-
market stocked.

By that time, I had taken the PSAT test. Fat, glossy
college catalogs came daily in the mail. Many of these fea-
tured happy, pretty people just a little older than I was,
eating in their dining halls with no adult supervision. The
food looked great!

> *"Once I had recognized the taste of the crumb of
> madeleine soaked in the decoction of lime flowers which
> my aunt used to give me, immediately the old gray
> house upon the street, where her room was, rose up like
> the scenery of a theater . . ."*

Proust made a bigger deal of all this than anyone, of
course—a twenty-three-hundred-page, seven-novel cycle

set in motion (and brought to closure) by a soggy cookie crumb, the definitive testimony to food's evocative, transporting power: a power greater than music, greater than photographs, greater than carefully stowed old clothes, maybe greater than anything. (Its only rival, smell, is taste's kissin' cousin.) I used to think that Proust just had a grotesque advantage over the rest of us, being French and all. I mean, lordylordylordy: *a decoction of lime flowers?* You go, Marcel. Me, I had to look up "decoction" in the dictionary. I'd context-guessed that it was sort of like "concoction," but really it means "an extract of flavor obtained by boiling." I'm pretty sure nobody in my family ever decocted anything, unless Jell-O counts.

But here's a kick in the head: Turns out, Proust's method works for everybody, as the essays in this book prove. Essays by gourmets and gourmands, by a self-proclaimed "picky eater," and by a self-proclaimed "non-gourmet." Essays by writers American-born and by culinary blessed first-generation immigrants. Essays about good food and bad. Essays about cooking and about eating. Essays about continental food, pan-Caribbean food, comfort food, Chinese food, southern food, and things (warning! the book you are holding contains an essay about eating brains!) that hardly seem like food at all. To write about what you ate (or drank), past tense, is to dream the past alive.

Think about it yourself. Think about the food served in the church basement right after your mother's funeral.

Not the funeral, just that sweet ham. Think about what you ate that one forlorn Christmas you had Christmas dinner at a $2.99 Las Vegas casino buffet. Not that Christmas, just that plate heaped with self-ladled stuffing. Think about the mud pie the neighborhood bully made you actually eat. Not Fat Clint, just the mouthful of oily dirt.

Taste it. Swallow. Close your eyes. Roll your tongue around in your mouth. You're *there*.

If you spent four years of poverty (or graduate school, or alcoholism) eating nothing but rice and beans, you can't talk about eating that without talking honestly about those four years. If a cherished part of the summers of your childhood was spent eating a postnuclear flavored Sno-kone, or participating face-first in the village pie-eating contest, then to celebrate the Sno-kone or to remember the taste of that supermarket-baked pie is to conjure up more than desserts of yore. If you can't eat shrimp scampi anymore because it was what your ex-spouse always, always ordered, a disquisition on shrimp scampi will, I guarantee you, produce not just a flood of memory, but more honest autobiography than will any earnestly straightforward attempt at honest autobiography.

For about a decade now, Share Our Strength has been publishing books, fiction and nonfiction alike, which, like this one, feature a couple dozen of the finest writers in America, all of whom have agreed to donate all royalties to fight the national disgrace of hunger (which, even more

disgracefully, in the face of what we are told is a time of unprecedented national prosperity, is on the increase). In addition S.O.S. has, since 1992, sponsored Writers Harvest, a nationwide fiction and poetry reading held one day each fall at several hundred different locations, which now raises nearly a quarter-million dollars a year.

I organized a reading the first year of Writers Harvest, and ever since have been passionately involved in it, on both local and national levels.

Why? Why this cause?

That can be a tough one to answer. (Speaking of France, did Jerry Lewis ever say what it is about muscular dystrophy?) A part of it for me is S.O.S. itself, a smart, lean, creative, low-overhead organization. I like the people who work there.

But why hunger?

Look at me: I'm built like a clumsy linebacker gone to seed. I was born to large American appetites. I do not watch what I eat. I take intense, essentially harmless pleasure in a fine meal. It sickens me to think that there are people out there, near me wherever I go, who are hungry. Most of them are children.

Yeah, well, that's me.

But why should other writers line up for *this* worthy cause as opposed to some other—whale-saving, say, or Tibetan liberation, or the Girl Scouts of America?

I thought my best answer came one summer when I

went to Denver for Share Our Strength's annual confer-
ence and heard a lecture by Dr. Larry Brown, an eminent
nutritionist, who explained how the human body has a way
of prioritizing energy so that the most basic functions
(eating, sleeping, eliminating) come first. If anything dis-
rupts that, the body shuts down. A life of the mind is, in
the most literal sense, a luxury. So is love. So is what we
think of as a human soul. Biology decrees: A perpetually
hungry person can't have these.

Gets worse.

Children, again the preponderance of the world's
hungry, can recover physically from severe childhood
malnutrition—but not mentally. Early childhood brain
development, if impeded by chronic malnutrition, is ir-
reversible.

If a writer wants to be read, if a writer wants a world in
which ideas and art are respected and appreciated, he or
she had better start out with a world in which kids get
enough to eat. That's square one, wordsmiths.

All of that is true, I guess.

But then I read Proust.

And that's where the idea for this book came from.

That's not exactly true.

Here's where the idea for this book really came from.

My sister is a teacher. A real teacher, middle school,
not a college professor like me. Late one night, I got a

phone call from her. She had an uncharacteristic edge to her voice.

"What are our ethnic traditions?" She sounded like she was reading this. "What are the foods and customs that have shaped our family's heritage?"

"You sound like you're reading this," I said.

"I sort of am," she said. She teaches in a huge county school system in suburban Washington, D.C., and she was taking a teacher-training in-service class, some state-mandated thing about ethnic sensitivity. "I have to give a presentation about this," she said.

The enormity of this was clear. We have no ethnicity. We grew up in a place as flavorless as the food we ate there and the times during which we ate it.

"You're screwed," I said. "Make stuff up."

"Exactly," she said. "Help me make stuff up."

This is what happens to you when you are the fiction writer in the family.

I can't remember what we made up. It was not inspired material, owing both to the lateness of the hour and also the dismal, unspoken realization that we look ineluctably like people who grew up where and how we did.

(Why, at least, didn't we think of the way food cemented the bond between *us?* While I was away at college, she started doing most of the cooking. Oregano and basil first entered the house. Finally, too, onions and garlic. I came home and things were different in every way. "Chili"

was actually replaced by chili [mild, but still]. "Casseroles" were replaced by actual food: lasagna! manicotti! ziti! [So what if Velveeta was involved? A corner had been turned.] That summer I was a lifeguard and a swimming-team coach at the public pool in the park across the street from my house. Swimming practice ended, the pool opened, and I didn't have time for lunch. Shari, one of the team's star swimmers, brought it to me. *Hot* lunches. She did not seem to mind, in fact seemed to enjoy, cooking that food and walking it over. I didn't mind driving her places. The four-year gap between us melted into inconsequence. That was the summer my sister and I became friends.)

Suddenly (I had been drinking), I came up with an idea. It's more or less what you've already read.

"Tell them about the soul food of our oppressed people!" I said. I was on a roll. "Learn it to the young-uns!"

"Have you been drinking?" she said.

"A little," I confessed.

"I'm serious," she said. "This presentation is next week."

(Right there you have it, the difference between us: I would have made a panicky call about a thing like this the night before it was due. Note to my students: I hate people like me.)

A week later, she got up in front of her class (she followed a middle-school art teacher whose mother was

African American and whose father was a full-blooded Cherokee) and began with the line, "I grew up in a house that never had an onion in it." People laughed like hell. No one believed her, she told me later. They thought they were laughing *with* her.

I am writing this on the first floor of a stone-and-stucco house at a place called Yaddo, in upstate New York. I've been here a month. Snow falls. It's about six o'clock on the night before the night before Christmas. Late tomorrow morning a taxi will come to pick me up and take me to the airport to fly home. (Soon after I get there, first my parents and then my sister and her family will arrive. For a week, then, our every move will be suffused with planning the next meal—as often as not, before the previous meal is even entirely eaten. One family tradition is for me to make a spitefully spicy chili, and my parents will find diplomatic ways to say they hate it; what no one knows is that this year I am, at thirty-six, finally mature enough to whip up a mild batch.) Home is now Tallahassee, Florida. Regional cuisine there is boiled peanuts and smoked mullet. Also fried gator tail. I've only lived there for a few months. None of this has taken.

(In truth, it hasn't taken with most anybody. Boiled peanuts, smoked mullet, and fried gator tail are novelty cuisine, which, except in the state of Louisiana, is about all that's left of regional cuisine. In most of American

nowhere—and America gets no more nowhere than Florida—regional cuisine and local custom have been franchised into nothingness, where every day is like TGIFriday's. In this respect, I was born and raised so that I might grow up and move to live among the strip malls of Florida.)

At Yaddo *everything* revolves around food. The food here is plentiful and exquisite (last night, an amazing sea bass; tonight, I don't know, but I snuck by and was wowed silly—curry is involved), though the real blessing is the way food provides each day's productively self-indulgent structure.

All over this august, snow-draped place, in the various stone cottages and frame houses that dot the pine woods, writers write and painters paint and sculptors sculpt and composers compose and choreographers choreograph and filmmakers make films. (Occasionally people catnap.) This is nice. But here's what's really important: The cook is cooking. I am not being glib. That's what's important: At six-thirty we will all convene for dinner.

You come to a place like this to work harder, with better focus and fewer distractions, than at home. But nothing—not even eradicating from your life the phone, or TV, or e-mail, or the quotidian errands that make up life (*brevis*) and kill art (*longa*)—matters more than the food. If I were home now, I'd stop writing. I've been working on this essay for a long time and I'm tired and I'd probably

just start dinner (or more likely I would call my wife and then one of us would go to the store and forage, or else we'd go out, maybe to a franchised restaurant). But I *can't* start dinner. Dinner starts at six-thirty, today and every day. I have nothing to do between now and then but write.

Years from now I suspect that I will have to stop and think which hundred-page section of my next novel was written here. I won't be able to describe the splendidly dowdy-aunt interior of this room. I will not be able to remember what shirts I wore here. *Maybe*, if I am lucky, I will still be in touch with some of the friends I made here.

But for the rest of my life, whenever I taste sea bass, I'll be back here.

Whenever I see a black plastic lunch pail or a waxed-paper packet full of carrot sticks, I will think of these artists, trudging each snowy morning from the dining hall, where breakfast had just been served (I ate oatmeal every morning; I hadn't had oatmeal for twenty years), to their studios, a Thermos of coffee in one hand, a winningly blue-collar black lunch pail in the other. Inside, the sandwiches and cookies vary. Some days there is couscous infused with golden raisins and grilled pine nuts. *Always* there are carrot sticks. Every day I happily ate them all, but I am sure that it will be a long time, after I eat the lunch I'll take with me on the plane tomorrow, before I eat another carrot stick.

I close my eyes. I swallow. I roll my tongue around in my mouth.

Carrot sticks. *Taste.*

Garlic-rubbed sea bass. *Taste.*

Whey-cheese lasagna. *Taste.*

Tuna fish stir-in "casserole." *Taste.*

Decoction of lime Jell-O. *Taste.*

Stale chili powder. *Taste.*

Brown the meat. *Taste.*

Raw (!) onion (!!) sprinkled over a fantasy of my most *habañero*-throttled chili. *Taste.*

Taste, Smell. Take. Eat.

I am *there.*

Good lord, look at the time.

C'mon. Time to go eat.

Picky Eater

I met my husband in my late thirties and when we were beginning to date I was surprised by his preoccupation with food. "Can we go out to dinner?" was, I believe, the second or third sentence out of his mouth. That first date we ate at a local restaurant, or I should say, he ate and talked, and I talked and picked at my food. "Didn't you like your stir-fry?" he asked me when the waitress removed my half-eaten meal.

"Sure, it was okay," I said, surprised at this non sequitur. We had been talking about India, where he had recently done volunteer surgery. I hadn't given the food a thought—except in ordering it. Being a picky eater, my

one criterion for food was: Is it something I might eat? Once it met that standard, then it was okay, nothing to think or talk too much about.

Mostly, if I was eating out, I didn't expect food to taste all that good. This was a carryover from my childhood in a big Dominican family in which the women prided themselves on the fact that nobody could put a meal on the table like they could put a meal on a table. You went out for the special purpose of seeing and being seen by your friends and neighbors, but you never went out to have a good meal. For that, you stayed home or went over to a relative's house where you could be sure that the food was going to be prepared correctly—that is, hygienically—and taste delicious.

Perhaps this bias had to do with the fact that I grew up in the 1950s in a small underdeveloped country where there were very few tourists and, therefore, few eating establishments that catered to pleasure dining. The common *comedores* were no-nonsense, one-room eating places for workers, mostly male, who all ate the same "plate of the day" on long tables, with small sinks and towels in a corner for washing their hands, and toothpicks for cleaning out their teeth when they were done. Little stands on the street sold fried *pastelitos* or *frío-frío* in paper cones or chunks of *raspadura* wrapped in palm leaves, treats I was never allowed to taste.

Eating *en la calle* was strictly forbidden in my family.

We came home from school at noon for the main dinner meal. On long trips into the interior to visit Papi's family, we carried everything we might need on the way, including water. It was dangerous to eat out: You could get very sick and die from eating foods that had gone bad or been fixed by people who had diseases you could catch. In fact, the minute any of us children complained we didn't feel right, the first question asked of our nursemaids was, "Did they eat anything on the street?"

My mothers and aunts were extremely careful about food preparation. Had the vegetables been properly peeled and boiled so that no *microbios* were left lodged in the skins? Was the lettuce washed in filtered water? Since electricity, and therefore refrigeration, were not dependable, was the meat fresh or had it been left to lie around? During certain seasons in the Tropics, some kinds of fish carry toxins—so that had to be taken into account as well. Had the milk been pasteurized? Had tarantulas gotten into the sugar or red ants into the cocoa powder? To get a healthy meal on the table seemed to be an enterprise laden with mythic dangers—no wonder a street vendor couldn't be trusted.

In short, I cannot remember ever eating out at a restaurant before coming to live in this country. The one exception was La Cremita, the ice cream shop that had recently opened up near the hospital. On Sundays, after we'd accompanied him on his rounds, my father took my

sisters and me to La Cremita where we picked out one small scoop apiece of our favorite *helado*. "Don't tell your mother," my father would say. I don't know if he was worried that my mother would accuse him of ruining our appetites before the big Sunday afternoon meal at my grandparents' house or if he was afraid she would fuss at him for exposing us to who-knows-what *microbios* the owners might have put into those big vats of pistachio or coconut or mango ice cream.

But even when we ate perfectly good, perfectly healthy food at home, my sisters and I were picky eaters. I remember long postmeal scenes, sitting in front of a plate of cold food that I had to finish. One "solution" my mother came up with was a disgusting milk drink, which she called *engrudo*, a name still synonymous in our extended family with my mother's strictness. Whatever my sisters and I left on our plates was ground up and put in a mixer with milk. This tall glass of greenish-brown liquid was then placed before us at the table. We were given a deadline: five minutes, ten minutes. (It seemed hours.) At the end of that time if we had not drunk up our *engrudos*, we were marched off to our rooms to do time until my father came home.

I have to say in my mother's defense that my sisters and I were very skinny and not always healthy. One sister had a heart ailment. Another had polio as a young child. I myself lost most of my hair at age three from a mysterious

malady. The doctors finally diagnosed it as "stress."
(Probably from having to drink *engrudos!*) My mother
worried herself sick (literally; bad migraines) that her chil-
dren would not make it through childhood. In a country
where the infant mortality was shockingly high, this was
not an irrational worry. Of course, most of these young
deaths tended to be among the poor who lacked proper
nutrition and medical care. Still, in my father's own family,
only one of his first ten siblings survived into adulthood.

And so childhood meals at home were battlegrounds.
And even if you won the dinner battle, refusing to clean
your plate or drink your *engrudo*, you inevitably lost the
war. When Papi came home, noneaters got shots. This is
not as sinister as it sounds: The shots, it turns out, were
"vitamin shots," B12 and liver, which really were for "our
own good." But to this day, every time I go to the doctor
and have to have blood drawn, I feel a vague sense that I
am being punished for not taking better care of myself.

Once we came to this country, the tradition of family
meals stopped altogether. We were suddenly too busy to
eat together as a family. Breakfasts were catch-as-catch-
can before running down the six or seven blocks to school.
We kept forgetting our lunches, so Mami finally gave up
and doled out lunch money to buy what we wanted. What
we wanted was the "junk food" we had never before been
allowed to eat. My sisters and I started putting on weight.
I think we all gained five or ten pounds that first year.

Suddenly I had leg and thigh and arm muscles I could flex! But what good were they when there were no cousins to show them off to? As for dinner—now that Papi was working so hard and got home late at night, we couldn't have this meal together, either. My sisters and I ate earlier, whenever the food was done. When Papi got home he ate alone in the kitchen, my mother standing by the stove warming up a pot of this or that for him.

In a few years, when my father's practice was doing better, he started coming home in time to join us for dinner. Actually he had shifted his hours around so that, instead of staying at the office late at night, he opened at five-thirty in the morning. This way his patients, many of them Latinos with jobs in *factorías*, could see the doctor before going to work on the first shift. Since Papi had to get up at four-thirty, so he could dress, have breakfast, and drive the half hour or so to Brooklyn, we ate dinner the minute he got home. As soon as he finished eating, my father would go upstairs and get ready for bed.

My mother and my sisters and I stayed behind at the table, Mami eating her Hershey bars—she'd pack in two or three a night, but then put Sweet'n Low in her *cafecito!* Now that her daughters were in the full, feisty bloom of adolescent health, she no longer worried over our eating habits or got insulted if we didn't eat her cooking. She had brought up a maid from the island to do the housework, so she could spend the day helping Papi out at his *oficina.*

Lunch was take-out from a little bodega down the street. It was safe to eat out now. This was America. People could be put in jail for fixing your food without a hair net or serving you something rotten that made you sick to your stomach.

The family plan had always been to go back home once the dictatorship had been toppled. But after Trujillo's assassination in 1961, politics on the island remained so unstable that my parents decided to stay "for now." My sisters and I were shipped off to boarding school, where meals again became fraught with performance pressures. We ate at assigned tables, with a teacher, a senior hostess, and six other girls. The point was to practice "conversational skills" while also learning to politely eat the worst food in the world. Everything seemed boiled to bland overdoneness. And the worst part of it was that, as in childhood, we had to eat a little serving of everything, unless we had a medical excuse. My father, who was still as much of a spoiler as back in his La Cremita days, agreed to let me fill in the infirmary form that asked if we had any special allergies or needs. I put down that I was allergic to mayonnaise, brussels sprouts, and most meats. No one, thank God, challenged me.

In college, in the height of the sixties, I finally achieved liberation from monitored eating. Students had to be on the meal plan, unless they had special dietary needs. A group of my friends applied to cook their own

macrobiotic meals in a college house kitchen, and I joined them. I soon discovered vegetarianism was a picky eater's godsend. You could be fussy *and* high-minded. Most meats were on my inedible list already, and mayonnaise was out for macrobiotics, who couldn't eat eggs. As for brussels spouts, they were an establishment vegetable like parsnips or cauliflower, something our parents might eat as an accompaniment to their meat.

All through my twenties and thirties as a mostly single woman, my idea of a meal was cheese and crackers or a salad with anything else I had lying around thrown in. I don't think I ever used the oven in my many rentals, except when the heat wasn't working. As for cooking, I could "fix" a meal, i.e., wash lettuce, open a can, or melt cheese on something in a frying pan, but that was about the extent of it. The transformations and alchemy recorded in cookbooks were as mysterious to me as a chemistry lab assignment. Besides, once I got a soufflé or a lasagna out of the oven, what was I supposed to do with it? Eat it all by myself? No, I'd rather take a package of crackers and a hunk of cheese with me in my knapsack to work. For an appetizer, why not a cigarette, and for dessert, some gum?

When I had friends over, a meal was never the context. Some other pretext was—listening to music, reading a new poetry book together, drinking a cup of coffee or a bottle of wine, munching on some more cheese and crackers. I'd clear off the dining table, which I had been using

as my desk, to hold this feast of bottles and boxes and packages and ashtrays.

Had I had a family I would no doubt have learned how to cook persuasive, tasty meals my children would eat. I would have worried about nutrition. I would have learned to knit the family together with food and talk. But just for myself, I couldn't be bothered. Cooking took time. Food cost money. I was too busy running around, earning a living, moving from job to low-paying job. Sometimes I lived in boarding houses where I didn't even have access to a kitchen. I grew as thin in my twenties and thirties as I had been as a child. My mother began to worry again about my eating. Maybe I had a touch of that anorexia disease American girls were increasingly getting.

"No," I protested, shades of *engrudo* lurking in my head. I preferred to think of myself as a picky eater. But probably all these bad eating habits and attitudes are "kissing cousins." Eating is dislodged from its nurturing purpose and becomes a metaphor for some struggle or other. My own experience with food had always been fraught with performance or punishment pressures. No wonder I didn't enjoy it, didn't want to deal with it, didn't want to cook it or even serve it. (My one waitressing job lasted less than a week. I kept forgetting what people had ordered and bringing them the wrong things.)

Of course, there was a way in which my whole apprehensive approach to food fell right in with the American

obsession with diets and fear of food additives and weight gain. As a child I had never heard of diets, except as something that people who were ill were put on. It was true that women sometimes said they were watching their figure, but it was vain and rude to stick to a diet when someone had gone to the trouble of putting some tasty dish on the table before you. The story is still told of my coquettish great-grandmother who was always watching her "little waist." She would resolve to keep a strict diet—only one meal per day—but then, approaching the table, she would invariably be tempted by an appetizing dish. "Well," she'd say, "I'm going to have lunch but I'll skip supper." At supper, she again couldn't resist what was on the table. "Well," she'd say, "I'm going to have a little supper, but I'll skip breakfast." By the time she died in her nineties, she owed hundreds upon hundred of skipped meals.

And so when at thirty-nine I married a doctor who was very involved with food and food preparation, I seemed to be returning to the scene of earlier emotional traumas to settle some score or exorcise some demon. A divorced father with two teenage daughters, my new husband had learned to cook out of necessity. Since his boyhood on a farm in Nebraska, he had always been involved in growing food, but the responsibility of being a single parent to two girls had turned him into a chef. Enter: one picky eater.

"What would you like to eat tonight?" my husband would ask me over the phone when he called me at lunch from his office. "I don't know," I'd say. Did I really have to make up my mind now about what I was going to eat in seven or eight hours?

With all this food planning and preparation going on around me I started to worry that I was not pulling my share. One night I announced that I thought we should each make dinner every other night. My husband looked worried. The one time I had invited him over to my house for dinner before we were married, I had served him a salad with bottled dressing and a side plate of fried onions and tofu squirted with chili sauce. This is a story my husband likes to tell a lot. I am always aggrieved that he forgets the dinner rolls, which I bought at the Grand Union bakery, something I would normally not do, since I much preferred crackers as "the bread" with my dinner.

But he liked doing the nightly cooking, he explained. It was his way to relax after a day at the office. Why not just help him out? I could do the shopping, which he didn't like to do. It turned out that he had to be very specific about what he put on the list or I would get "the wrong thing": baking powder instead of baking soda, margarine instead of butter. "You're so picky!" I would say, not always immediately aware of the irony. One stick of yellow grease was so much like another.

I also helped with making dinner, though he gave me so little to do beyond washing the lettuce and keeping him company while he did the rest, that I began to suspect he didn't trust me even to help. Finally, we agreed that I would be in charge of making the desserts. For months we had brownies, which were really quite good when I remembered to put the sugar in.

Meals, which had been something I did while doing something else, now took up big blocks of time, especially on Sundays, when Bill's parents came over for dinner. First, we had soup, and then when we were done with the soup, several platters made the rounds, and then there was dessert. Then coffee. During all these courses there was much talk about what we were eating and other memorable variations of what was on the table. If you were to take one of those pies statisticians use to show percentages and were to cut out a serving that would represent how much of the time we talked about food, I would say you'd have to cut yourself at least half the pie, and probably a second serving before the night was over. It took so long to eat!

True, when I was a young girl, the weekly dinners in my grandparents' house were long, lingering family affairs, but that was true only for the adults. Once we children got through the chore of finishing what was on our plates, we would be excused to go play in the garden while

the grownups droned on over their everlasting courses and *cafecitos*. (No *engrudos* when we ate at somebody else's house!)

But now I was one of those adults at the table of a family that was obviously bound together, not at the hip, but the belly. Traditionally my husband's people have been farmers, intimately connected with food—growing it, serving it, preserving it, preparing it. As we lingered at the table, I listened, not understanding at first what the fuss was about. What was the difference between a Sungold tomato and a Big Boy? Why was sweet corn better than regular corn? What was the difference between a Yukon Gold and a baking potato? What did it mean when they said raspberries were "setting on"? And how come the second crop was always bigger, juicier?

Eventually I realized that if I ate slowly and kept my ears opened, I could learn a lot. I also started to taste the food, instead of swallowing it, and slowly I developed new criteria—not just would I eat it or not. Did the flavors work together? Was the polenta bland or the bread chewy enough? As my own cooking repertoire expanded beyond brownies, I discovered the wonderful pleasure of transforming a pile of ingredients into a recipe that nurtured and sometimes delighted the people I love. It was akin to writing a poem, after all.

Now, eight years into sharing our table, my husband and I have developed a fair and equitable cooking arrange-

ment. I am in charge of certain recipes—and not just desserts. I've even learned to cook certain meats for him and his parents, though I still don't eat them. For holidays, when the house is humming with beaters, hissing with steamers, beeping with oven timers, I feel the pulse of happiness whose center is the kitchen.

But I admit that years of picky eating don't vanish overnight. I still worry when we go out if there will be anything in the category of things-I-eat. There are still times when I come back from the kitchen and spy my husband and his family gathered at the table, talking away about the difference between this week's crust and last week's crust or how you can get the peak in those whipped potatoes or individual grains in the rice, and I wonder if I belong here. Will I ever stop feeling as if I've wandered into one of those Norman Rockwell scenes of a family sitting around a table laden with platters and pies? But each time I've put down what I had in my hands—my contribution to the feast—and looked around, I've found a place set for me at the table.

Onion Pie

I was offered a job as caretaker of a farmhouse in the south of France. My friend's legal troubles were well behind her, and since our on-again, off-again romance seemed to be on again, we decided to join forces and take the job together. We had both run out of money by then, and without this offer we would have been compelled to return to America--which neither one of us was prepared to do just yet.

It turned out to be a curious year. On the one hand, the place was beautiful: a large, eighteenth-century stone house bordered by vineyards on one side and a national forest on the other. The nearest village was two kilometers

away, but it was inhabited by no more than forty people, none of whom was under sixty or seventy years old. It was an ideal spot for two young writers to spend a year, and L. and I both worked hard there, accomplishing more in that house than either one of us would have thought possible.

On the other hand, we lived on the brink of permanent catastrophe. Our employers, an American couple who lived in Paris, sent us a small monthly salary (fifty dollars), a gas allowance for the car, and money to feed the two Labrador retrievers who were part of the household. All in all it was a generous arrangement. There was no rent to pay, and even if our salary fell short of what we needed to live on, it gave us a head start on each month's expenses. Our plan was to earn the rest by doing translations. Before leaving Paris and settling in the country, we had set up a number of jobs to see us through the year. What we had neglected to take into account was that publishers are often slow to pay their bills. We had also forgotten to consider that checks sent from one country to another can take weeks to clear, and that once they do, bank charges and exchange fees cut into the amounts of those checks. Since L. and I had left no margin for error or miscalculation, we often found ourselves in quite desperate straits.

I remember savage nicotine fits, my body numb with need as I scrounged among sofa cushions and crawled behind cupboards in search of loose coins. For eighteen

centimes (about three and a half cents) you could buy a
brand of cigarettes called Parisiennes, which were sold in
packs of four. I remember feeding the dogs and thinking
that they ate better than I did. I remember conversations
with L. when we seriously considered opening a can of
dog food and eating it for dinner.

Our only other source of income that year came from
a man named James Sugar. (I don't mean to insist on
metaphorical names, but facts are facts, and there's noth-
ing I can do about it.) Sugar worked as a staff photogra-
pher for *National Geographic*, and he entered our lives
because he was collaborating with one of our employers
on an article about the region. He took pictures for sev-
eral months, crisscrossing Provence in a rented car pro-
vided by his magazine, and whenever he was in our neck
of the woods he would spend the night with us. Since the
magazine also provided him with an expense account, he
would very graciously slip us the money that had been al-
lotted for his hotel costs. If I remember correctly, the sum
came to fifty francs a night. In effect, L. and I became his
private innkeepers, and since Sugar was an amiable man
into the bargain, we were always glad to see him. The only
problem was that we never knew when he was going to
turn up. He never called in advance, and more often than
not weeks would go by between his visits. We therefore
learned not to count on Mr. Sugar. He would arrive out of
nowhere, pulling up in front of the house in his shiny blue

car, stay for a night or two, and then disappear again. Each time he left we assumed that was the last time we would ever see him.

The worst moments came for us in the late winter and early spring. Checks failed to arrive, one of the dogs was stolen, and little by little we ate our way through the stockpile of food in the kitchen. In the end we had nothing left but a bag of onions, a bottle of cooking oil, and a packaged pie crust that someone had bought before we ever moved into the house—a stale remnant from the previous summer. L. and I held out all morning and into the afternoon, but by 2:30 hunger had gotten the better of us, and so we went into the kitchen to prepare our last meal. Given the paucity of elements we had to work with, an onion pie was the only dish that made sense.

After our concoction had been in the oven for what seemed a sufficient length of time, we took it out, set it on the table, and dug in. Against all our expectations, we both found it delicious. I think we even went so far as to say that it was the best food we had ever tasted, but no doubt that was a ruse, a feeble attempt to keep our spirits up. Once we had chewed a little more, however, disappointment set in. Reluctantly—ever so reluctantly—we were forced to admit that the pie had not yet cooked through, that the center was still too cold to eat. There was nothing to be done but put it back in the oven for another ten or fifteen minutes. Considering how hungry we were, and

considering that our salivary glands had just been acti-
vated, relinquishing the pie was not easy.

To stifle our impatience we went outside for a brief
stroll, thinking the time would pass more quickly if we re-
moved ourselves from the good smells in the kitchen. As I
remember it, we circled the house once, perhaps twice.
Perhaps we drifted into a deep conversation about some-
thing (I can't remember), but however it happened, and
however long we were gone, by the time we entered the
house again the kitchen was filled with smoke. We rushed
to the oven and pulled out the pie, but it was too late. Our
meal was dead. It had been incinerated, burned to a
charred and blackened mass, and not one morsel could be
salvaged.

It sounds like a funny story now, but at the time it was
anything but funny. We had fallen into a dark hole, and
neither one of us could think of a way to get out. In all my
years of struggling to be a man, I doubt there has ever
been a moment when I felt less inclined to laugh or crack
jokes. This was really the end, and it was a terrible and
frightening place to be.

That was at four o'clock in the afternoon. Less than
an hour later, the errant Mr. Sugar suddenly appeared,
driving up to the house in a cloud of dust, gravel and dirt
crunching all around him. If I think about it hard enough,
I can still see the naive and goofy smile on his face as he
bounced out of the car and said hello. It was a miracle. It

was a genuine miracle, and I was there to witness it with my own eyes, to live it in my own flesh. Until that moment, I had thought those things happened only in books.

Sugar treated us to dinner that night in a two-star restaurant. We ate copiously and well, we emptied several bottles of wine, we laughed our heads off. And yet, delicious as that food must have been, I can't remember a thing about it. But I have never forgotten the taste of the onion pie.

My Son, Eating Dinner

We've all seen the stereotype, usually in the movies: a large Italian mama, apron wrapping her considerable figure, waddles through the grimy working-class kitchen and dining room, waving, in her pudgy hands, a wooden pasta server at her cowering adult son or daughter. She shouts, "Eat! Eat!" Spaghetti sauce flecks off the implement and spatters the wall and the linoleum floor. "Look at you! You'll starve!" she says.

Laughter arises from the audience. The adult we see is in no danger of starving. This woman is in the grip of a mania.

For myself, I have no emotions about the food I shovel into my mouth. I am what might be called an anti-gourmet, or perhaps just a non-gourmet, a man whose palate has never been educated or trained or advanced toward the higher delicacies, and like most anti-gourmets, I eat almost anything, mindlessly and gnomishly. I pay no attention to what I'm doing when I eat and am a champion spiller. Every shirt of mine, as it goes into the wash, is decorated with food stains. I am something of an embarrassment in polite company. I happen to enjoy fast food almost as much as well-prepared and subtly seasoned epicurean dishes. Egg salad or quiche? Don't care. I generally don't notice what I eat (a good adaptive habit of mind for anyone living in the Midwest), and though the qualities of a fine meal are not lost on me—I'm not a *total* philistine in these matters—for much of the time I am simply oblivious. I am more alert to the coffee I drink than I am to any matters of nutrition or the palate. "Palate"! I don't even like the *word*.

Until my son was born, I never bothered to learn how to cook. Edible objects got themselves boiled or fried or broiled on my stove. As someone (a college friend) once observed, abruptly and rather ungraciously, when I served him one of my meals, "That's not cooking. You've just heated things up."

I've always been an expert at washing dishes, however. Washing dishes is the paradise of daydreaming.

Writers tend to be good at getting their hands wet and soapy.

The night our son was born, he came out of his mother coated with "celestial cheesiness," to use Galway Kinnell's wonderful phrase from *The Book of Nightmares*. For several days following his birth, he was a dead ringer for my father-in-law. He had that ancient look some infants have, the strange visual cross-hatching between infancy and late middle age. In the close-up photographs of him, taken when he was a week old, he has the solemn and contented look of a man smoking a fine Havana cigar.

But that expression didn't last. He didn't nurse well, and soon after his birth something seemed to be going wrong with his sucking reflex. Barely six pounds when he was born, he subsequently lost weight and was jaundiced. When he began to breast-feed he was an irritable and unpredictable baby, tormented by colic every hour of the day and night.

The books and our friends and relatives said the colic would go away. Everyone claimed that eventually he would start to sleep through the night. But when his colic didn't disappear, our pediatrician began to prescribe paregoric as a topical remedy. This at least is my memory of what happened.

Night after night, week after week, he would cry and scream. He was hungry. So he would nurse. Then fifteen

or twenty minutes later he would begin, agonizingly, to wail again. And sometimes we would medicate him with the narcotic.

We went to another pediatrician, who diagnosed the problem as lactose intolerance. By this time our son was beginning to look like a "failure-to-thrive" child, to use a scarifying phrase. He wasn't wasting away, but he wasn't growing, and he had a painfully scrawny look. He sometimes seemed a bit hollow-eyed. He dropped off the development charts.

As is sometimes the case with Asian or Jewish children and adults (my wife is Jewish), the body apparently does not produce the necessary enzymes for digesting milk. On the doctor's recommendation we put our son on soy formula and promptly found that he was unable to tolerate that, as well. He woke up four or five times a night. We would try to feed him, but what he was eating appeared to hurt him; he would start crying again and his body would seem to be gripped by a terrible interior clamp. This went on for months.

Most parents have created paths in the carpeting or tracks on the floor from walking their colicky babies to-and-fro across the living room or bedroom. We did, too. All I could think of, walking him everywhere in the house, was: *If only there were something he could eat that wouldn't hurt*

him. As it happens, there was, but we weren't alerted to it until our son was over a year old. In the meantime I sometimes felt that my son was starving, that if he didn't find a food that agreed with him, he would become seriously malnourished, with all the consequences that follow.

We found a formula—an engineered product available by prescription with simpler, smaller molecules easily absorbed into a baby's digestive tract—and slowly he grew, developed, prospered, in his way. He didn't, however, sleep through the night until he was four. Many foods disagreed with him and made him sick. We would find certain other foods—oatmeal, ground lamb, sweet potatoes—that he could tolerate, and we would feed him these substances until he developed an intolerance for them. I began to feel, when he was around seven years old, that maybe we were out of the woods.

But my story is not really about a baby with eating difficulties. Because, look: Here he is now, eighteen years old, almost nineteen, with plans to be a civil engineer, home from college during the winter break, shuffling off to his job at the photo department at Meijer Thrifty Acres, looking forward to his time off when he can play music with his friends in the band they've formed, The School of Velocity (tapes available by mail order, c/o the undersigned). He likes to sleep late. His room is a mess. He writes his own music, he's doing fine in school, he's still a picky eater—is

that so different from other teenagers?—and the story would end there, except that his infancy left a trace, a shadow in me that I will never get over.

I discovered that the emotion I lacked in putting food into my own mouth arose in great quantity when I was feeding my son. In a strange way, that has persisted. I became passionate about food, not for me, but for him. When I did so, I remembered, in a degraded Proustian way, that I myself had been a poor eater, scrawny and anemic, underweight, off the charts, a worry to my own parents, and in order to get me to eat, my mother had placed food on spoons and pretended that, in her hand, they were flying through the air on a dangerous mission through turbulence in order to get to my mouth, which I was supposed to open to let the food inside. And so it did. My mouth opened, I ate. I relieved my parent of her anxiety that I would starve. I learned to eat regularly until I was eight years old, when I thought I was unable to swallow and stopped eating solid food for a few weeks.

Years later, when I was feeding my son, I had the soul of a fat Italian mama. I was thinking, "Eat, eat!" When his mouth opened and the spoon laden with oatmeal or apple sauce made its way in, I felt a short breath, a sigh of relief. I myself made the spoon fly in the air, in turbulence, around the table and in front of him, on its dangerous mission toward him. Later when he developed a taste for

McDonald's hamburgers (just the meat, never the buns, and now, years later, still no pickle), around the age of four, and when it became apparent that these hamburgers didn't hurt him and that they were nutritious besides, every political idea I had ever had about McDonald's and their wastefulness, their destruction of the rain forests, their deplorable labor practices, their generally gruesome food, went sailing out the window. Their food was keeping my son alive, and I blessed them in my heart.

I am not doing a particularly good job of teaching my son to cook because, whenever he's come from college, I like to prepare dishes for him, meals he likes: salads and pastas, especially. I realize now that the reason I never learned to cook as an adolescent or young man was that my parents were so anxious about my failure to thrive that they always had food available for me. One step toward the kitchen, and somebody would warm up some dish (often a terrible leftover, but so what?) for my benefit and put it in front of me.

To have a sickly child, or an ailing friend or relative or partner, and to be beside that person, holding a spoon in the hand and asking him or her to open up and to eat, returns food from its place as an artifice of the chefs to a substance of survival. You begin to count spoonfuls. You make guesses about calories and nutrients and food groups. You feel like weeping with happiness if an entire

meal stays down. You internalize an appetite that the person you love does not seem to have. It is a will to live that you are conveying, on small spoons and forks.

One other consequence of all this: I am not particularly squeamish but I now find that I am virtually unable to look at photographs of those who are malnourished, and as for malnourished children, no, I cannot look and can barely bring myself to think about them, except when I am making some effort or other for hunger relief. It doesn't feel political so much as personal.

Tonight, Sunday, it's spaghetti night, and though he's off at his job, I will make spaghetti for myself, because that's what he always expected on Sunday once he was in the upper grades, and old habits die hard. We would make great heaping quantities of it and he would eat so much of it that he would get sleepy after dinner sometimes. Once again, though, eating for myself alone, I have grown oblivious to what I'm doing. I talk or read or watch the news while shoveling the food inside. The evidence is on my shirts, but fortunately, because it's Sunday, they're being washed.

♪ ♪ ♪

Manje

January 1997

Food and the act of eating are the same word in Kreyol. The average Haitian thinks about this action rather more often than he or she is able to perform it. But Haitian cuisine, a synthesis of French and African ideas of food, is delicious if you have the purchase power. Good and pricey restaurants in Port-au-Prince, or the kitchens of the hotels for foreigners, provided subtly flavored soups; gamey and tasty meat from the well-exercised native pigs, goats, and chickens; a surprisingly succulent conch stew (known in Kreyol as *lambi*), piquantly seasoned with *habañero* peppers. There was a greater supply of fresh fish than had been available before the intervention (when anyone with

command of a boat immediately set sail for Florida), and on the north coast you even found a delicately flavored Haitian lobster.

If you were Haitian you would very seldom eat the foods that were served to *blancs*. You got by on *riz ak pois*, cassava bread, bananas, fruit, sticks of fresh-peeled sugar cane, and the root vegetables that, since slavery time, had been known as *vivres*. You ate meat seldom and in very small quantities; somewhat more frequently you might swallow rich soup stocks boiled from bones.

If you were *blanc* you could eat whatever you liked so long as you didn't mind getting dysentery, which would be inconvenient during long days of travel on Haitian roads, and in severe cases could lead to rectal hemorrhaging followed by death. Therefore you had to follow certain rules: principally that everything you ate must be well cooked and (what was more difficult to know) recently cooked, for if flies lit on the food after it had been prepared the same sorts of problems were likely to ensue. Sadly, the delicious-looking fruits were not worth the risk (unless you were assured of clean water to wash them before cutting), and we had to resist the delicious-smelling cassava bread that Xavier always bought at the roadside markets— it was still warm, but had been a little too frequently passed from hand to hand.

In Port-au-Prince you didn't need to worry—in the hotels for *blancs* it was probably even safe to eat a salad. If

you went north by the coast road, there were safe restaurants in the beach hotels and then at Gonaives. But the interior was unknown territory concerning *manje sauf pou blanc*, so you ate infrequently, perhaps once a day, cautiously even then, and not too much. This taught you something about hunger, and something about organizing food—for perhaps the majority of Haitians the whole day's energy went into organizing the materials for a single meager meal. On the return flight the American doctor remarked to me that she found it strange how Haitian adults always ate before their children, especially when in all other respects Haitians were so loving with their children. But of course, I explained to her, when there was absolutely no slack in anyone's situation, the adults must eat first so they would have energy to go out and stalk the ingredients for their family's next meal. We had to look away from each other then, the doctor and I, for it was not yet a suitable moment to begin weeping.

Later on, when you did get somewhat sick in spite of all precautions, you could eat almost nothing but rice (which absorbed toxins and cleansed the stomach), perhaps rice and beans if you felt sufficiently daring, but careful with beans—it was necessary to balance your need for protein with the risk of worsening your illness. Once you returned from the interior to the establishments frequented by *blancs*, you could look at all sorts of interesting food without actually being able to eat it. At Moulin Sur

Mer, a "vacation prison" similar to Club Med but less expensive and more attractively designed, there were hamburgers, club sandwiches, and sirloin steaks, rather expensive but certainly healthy (even the flies that wafted around the sea breeze seemed to have passed a health inspection), and yet your purchase power had ceased to be meaningful due to the condition of your intestines, so you must only eat a little *riz ak pois*, perhaps half a normal serving.

No matter what it was they were eating, Haitians always ate very slowly, deliberately, without conversation, chewing each mouthful with great care so that all nutrients would be extracted. They did not hurry, but in the end, when all the bones had been cracked and sucked, they left absolutely nothing at all. For somewhat different reasons you adopted the same manner of eating. A slow pace and very thorough chewing were certainly wiser for your stomach, and as for conversation, the culture shock of arriving at Moulin Sur Mer after days on the central plateau and *au* Cap had struck you speechless anyway. Here the international businessmen locked up their families in pleasant security, so the beach was scattered with young white mothers sunning in bikinis, and toddlers playing in the sand. The sun was tilting westward toward the island of Gonave and the flat, still surface of the bay was turned a coppery color by the light. A dugout Haitian sailboat plied toward Gonave, sail half-slackening from the mast.

Below the mirrored surface of the water was the Island Below Sea, the metaphysical Guinée, African home of Les Morts and Les Mystères, who could not rise up through that surface until Legba opened the way for their passage. Who were these people who sat stuporously on the sunny beach, without knowing anything of history or the gods? They were *blancs*, but what were you?

When so many people had so much trouble finding food, fat became the most ostentatious evidence of wealth. Body fat meant warm, comfortable, voluptuous prosperity. For this reason Alex was vastly admired by everyone. Cries of "*Gros nèg!*" (or in the capital, "Beeg Boy!") rang up and down the street whenever we took a stroll. The prostitutes who chased us down the Rue Capois from the Champ de Mars stroked his belly lovingly, not quite believing it was real. In the countryside, women wanted to make love with him for free.

But just at the moment, life for Haitians successful enough to be fat had become rather complicated and difficult. The skinny Haitians, meaning the vast majority, were angry about neoliberalism and structural adjustment and *la vie chère*, but just now they were most furious of all at the *grans manjes*—big eaters. That mood was feeding into the carnival season—this year's most popular carnival song was a denunciation of the *grans manjes*. Therefore it was not safe for fat people to show themselves in public. You could always exchange your Armani for a suit of rags

when you wanted to go slumming, but slipping out of sixty pounds of excess avoirdupois was quite another matter. For the time being, the fat Haitians kept behind the high walls of the fortresslike houses in enclaves like Petionville, or (more rarely) behind the tinted windows of their Mercedes Benzes.

In fact, the only heavy Haitians I ever saw (outside the airport) were the three gargantuan coal-black women who served the tables at the little restaurant of the Hotel Internationalle in Cap Haitien. The fat ladies were wonderfully generous with food—they would give you both legs of a chicken atop a gigantic heap of *riz ak pois*, with a bowl of rich gravy on the side. If you ate there slowly and carefully, according to the Haitian eating habits you had now adopted, you were nourished enough to hold on for two days.

When we arrived the choice was the chicken and rice or some sort of spaghetti concoction, and as I mistrusted the spaghetti, I said that I preferred *manje Ayitien*. One of the *gros mamans* looked at me coldly (truly those women always looked sullen but this was because their thick, fat cheeks squeezed their eyes into rather unpleasant expressions) and said, "Chicken is *not* a Haitian food." Whereupon I understood that her rolls of blubber were evidence not of greed or gluttony but of thrift—the lady's fat was her bank account.

The Haitians, meanwhile, had taken to eating some

rather odd things. Spaghetti with butter and ketchup had become very popular, perhaps because it was believed to be American food, perhaps only because it was cheap and high in carbohydrates. Ensure had evolved into a popular after-dinner drink. In the capital, all sorts of processed, packaged foods had become more common since the intervention—certainly this sort of thing kept better, and the packaging helped to make it safe.

For now, and for some time after you returned to the United States as well, you were better off with rice and a little beans, but not too much. If that did not teach you about being Haitian, at least you learned about hunger in the midst of plenty. Your attitude toward food would not revert to normal even when your intestinal complaint improved. When you went to the grocery store you were apt to fall into a sort of fugue state; there was too much, too many choices; it was impossible to choose, and you came near the brink of panic. You were allowed to eat whatever you needed, and there was no harm in making your food interesting and tasty, but overeating now felt truly shameful. Whenever you saw people wasting food, you pretty well wanted to kill them.

At Hinche we selected *gros bouillon*, which I figured was the safest bet since it would have been boiled a long time; besides, I had always wanted to try it. Under the light of a not-quite-full moon we walked to the restaurant where *gros bouillon* was prepared. Some forms of progress

had landed in Hinche from afar: the support mission had paved the central streets and square with durable-looking hexagonal blocks, and to counterbalance the Shell station surreally positioned on the perimeter, in the center there was a colossal church that also looked to have been dropped from a spaceship, magnificently domed and painted blue and white. The moonlight was so vague that our skin color did not seem remarkable; besides, everyone in town was solemnly concentrating on a news broadcast in Kreyol that seemed to play, stentoriously, from every door and window we passed. At the *gros bouillon* restaurant we were the first guests to arrive, and they wanted to turn on the electric lights for us, but I demurred—the dim interior was more pleasant and also gave us better camouflage.

Gros bouillon was a thick and yellow stock, floating with chunks of potato, plantain, yam, carrot, small cylindrical cassava-flour dumplings, and a few tiny and knotty pieces of goat meat that clung to shards of bone. After twenty hours without food the impact of this nourishment was indescribable. A single long table filled the whole space of the restaurant; we shared it with several small parties of Haitians who happened by. In the comforting darkness we ate slowly, silently, with profound respect; eating had become a form of prayer.

WENDELL BERRY

The Pleasures
of Eating

Many times, after I have finished a lecture on the decline
of American farming and rural life, someone in the audi-
ence has asked, "What can city people do?"

"Eat responsibly," I have usually answered. Of course,
I have tried to explain what I meant by that, but afterwards
I have invariably felt that there was more to be said than I
had been able to say. Now I would like to attempt a better
explanation.

I begin with the proposition that eating is an agricul-
tural act. Eating ends the annual drama of the food econ-
omy that begins with planting and birth. Most eaters,
however, are no longer aware that this is true. They think

of food as an agricultural product, perhaps, but they do not think of themselves as participants in agriculture. They think of themselves as "consumers." If they think beyond that, they recognize that they are passive consumers. They buy what they want—or what they have been persuaded to want—within the limits of what they can get. They pay, mostly without protest, what they are charged. And they mostly ignore certain critical questions about the quality and the cost of what they are sold: How fresh is it? How pure or clean is it, how free of dangerous chemicals? How far was it transported and what did transportation add to the cost? How much did manufacturing or packaging or advertising add to the cost? When the food product has been manufactured or "processed" or "precooked," how has that affected its quality or price or nutritional value?

Most urban shoppers would tell you that food is produced on farms. But most of them do not know what farms, or what kinds of farms, or where the farms are, or what knowledge or skills are involved in farming. They apparently have little doubt that farms will continue to produce, but they do not know how or over what obstacles. For them, then, food is pretty much an abstract idea—something they do not know or imagine—until it appears on the grocery shelf or on the table.

The specialization of production induces specialization of consumption. Patrons of the entertainment industry, for example, entertain themselves less and less and

have become more and more passively dependent on com-
mercial suppliers. This is certainly true also of patrons of
the food industry, who have tended more and more to be
mere consumers—passive, uncritical, and dependent. In-
deed, this sort of consumption may be said to be one of
the chief goals of industrial production. The food indus-
trialists have by now persuaded millions of consumers to
prefer food that is already prepared. They will grow, de-
liver, and cook your food for you and (just like your
mother) beg you to eat it. That they do not yet offer to in-
sert it, prechewed, into your mouth is only because they
have found no profitable way to do so. We may rest as-
sured that they would be glad to find such a way. The ideal
industrial food consumer would be strapped to a table
with a tube running from the food factory directly into his
or her stomach.

Perhaps I exaggerate, but not by much. The industrial
eater is, in fact, one who does not know that eating is an
agricultural act, who no longer knows or imagines the
connections between eating and the land, and who is
therefore necessarily passive and uncritical—in short, a
victim. When food, in the minds of eaters, is no longer as-
sociated with farming and with the land, then the eaters
are suffering a kind of cultural amnesia that is misleading
and dangerous. The current version of the "dream home"
of the future involves "effortless" shopping from a list of
available goods on a television monitor and heating pre-

cooked food by remote control. Of course, this implies and depends on a perfect ignorance of the history of the food that is consumed. It requires that the citizenry should give up their hereditary and sensible aversion to buying a pig in a poke. It wishes to make the selling of pigs in pokes an honorable and glamorous activity. The dreamer in this dream home will perforce know nothing about the kind or quality of this food, or where it came from, or how it was produced and prepared, or what ingredients, additives, and residues it contains—unless, that is, the dreamer undertakes a close and constant study of the food industry, in which case he or she might as well wake up and play an active and responsible part in the economy of food.

There is, then, a politics of food that, like any politics, involves our freedom. We still (sometimes) remember that we cannot be free if our minds and voices are controlled by someone else. But we have neglected to understand that we cannot be free if our food and its sources are controlled by someone else. The condition of the passive consumer of food is not a democratic condition. One reason to eat responsibly is to live free.

But if there is a food politics, there are also a food aesthetics and a food ethics, neither of which is dissociated from politics. Like industrial sex, industrial eating has become a degraded, poor, and paltry thing. Our kitchens and other eating places more and more resemble filling stations, as our homes more and more resemble motels.

"Life is not very interesting," we seem to have decided. "Let its satisfactions be minimal, perfunctory, and fast." We hurry through our meals to go to work and hurry through our work in order to "recreate" ourselves in the evenings and on weekends and vacations. And then we hurry, with the greatest possible speed and noise and violence, through our recreation—for what? To eat the billionth hamburger at some fast-food joint hell-bent on increasing the "quality" of our life? And all this is carried out in a remarkable obliviousness to the causes and effects, the possibilities and the purposes, of the life of the body in this world.

One will find this obliviousness represented in virgin purity in the advertisements of the food industry, in which food wears as much makeup as the actors. If one gained one's whole knowledge of food from these advertisements (as some presumably do), one would not know that the various edibles were ever living creatures, or that they all come from the soil, or that they were produced by work. The passive American consumer, sitting down to a meal of preprepared or fast food, confronts a platter covered with inert, anonymous substances that have been processed, dyed, breaded, sauced, gravied, ground, pulped, strained, blended, prettified, and sanitized beyond resemblance to any part of any creature that ever lived. The products of nature and agriculture have been made, to all appearances, the products of industry. Both eater and eaten are thus in

exile from biological reality. And the result is a kind of solitude, unprecedented in human experience, in which the eater may think of eating as, first, a purely commercial transaction between him and a supplier and then as a purely appetitive transaction between him and his food.

And this peculiar specialization of the act of eating is, again, of obvious benefit to the food industry, which has good reasons to obscure the connection between food and farming. It would not do for the consumer to know that the hamburger she is eating came from a steer who spent much of his life standing deep in his own excrement in a feedlot, helping to pollute the local streams, or that the calf that yielded the veal cutlet on her plate spent its life in a box in which it did not have room to turn around. And, though her sympathy for the slaw might be less tender, she should not be encouraged to meditate on the hygienic and biological implications of mile-square fields of cabbage, for vegetables grown in huge monocultures are dependent on toxic chemicals—just as animals in close confinement are dependent on antibiotics and other drugs.

The consumer, that is to say, must be kept from discovering that, in the food industry—as in any other industry—the overriding concerns are not quality and health, but volume and price. For decades now the entire industrial food economy, from the large farms and feedlots to the chains of supermarkets and fast-food restaurants, has been obsessed with volume. It has relentlessly increased scale in

order to increase volume in order (presumably) to reduce costs. But as scale increases, diversity declines; as diversity declines, so does health; as health declines, the dependence on drugs and chemicals necessarily increases. As capital replaces labor, it does so by substituting machines, drugs, and chemicals for human workers and for the natural health and fertility of the soil. The food is produced by any means or any shortcut that will increase profits. And the business of the cosmeticians of advertising is to persuade the consumer that food so produced is good, tasty, healthful, and a guarantee of marital fidelity and long life.

It is possible, then, to be liberated from the husbandry and wifery of the old household food economy. But one can be thus liberated only by entering a trap (unless one sees ignorance and helplessness as the signs of privilege, as many people apparently do). The trap is the ideal of industrialism: a walled city surrounded by valves that let merchandise in but no consciousness out. How does one escape this trap? Only voluntarily, the same way that one went in: by restoring one's consciousness of what is involved in eating; by reclaiming responsibility for one's own part in the food economy. One might begin with the illuminating principle of Sir Albert Howard's *The Soil and Health*, that we should understand "the whole problem of health in soil, plant, animal, and man as one great subject." Eaters, that is, must understand that eating takes place inescapably in the world, that it is inescapably an agricul-

tural act, and that how we eat determines, to a considerable extent, how the world is used. This is a simple way of describing a relationship that is inexpressibly complex. To eat responsibly is to understand and enact, so far as one can, this complex relationship. What can one do? Here is a list, probably not definitive:

1. Participate in food production to the extent that you can. If you have a yard or even just a porch box or a pot in a sunny window, grow something to eat in it. Make a little compost of your kitchen scraps and use it for fertilizer. Only by growing some food for yourself can you become acquainted with the beautiful energy cycle that revolves from soil to seed to flower to fruit to food to offal to decay, and around again. You will be fully responsible for any food that you grow for yourself, and you will know all about it. You will appreciate it fully, having known it all its life.

2. Prepare your own food. This means reviving in your own mind and life the arts of kitchen and household. This should enable you to eat more cheaply, and it will give you a measure of "quality control": You will have some reliable knowledge of what has been added to the food you eat.

3. Learn the origins of the food you buy, and buy the food that is produced closest to your home.

The idea that every locality should be, as much as possible, the source of its own food makes several kinds of sense. The locally produced food supply is the most secure, the freshest, and the easiest for local consumers to know about and to influence.

4. Whenever possible, deal directly with a local farmer, gardener, or orchardist. All the reasons listed for the previous suggestion apply here. In addition, by such dealing you eliminate the whole pack of merchants, transporters, processors, packagers, and advertisers who thrive at the expense of both producers and consumers.

5. Learn, in self-defense, as much as you can of the economy and technology of industrial food production. What is added to food that is not food, and what do you pay for these additions?

6. Learn what is involved in the *best* farming and gardening.

7. Learn as much as you can, by direct observation and experience if possible, of the life histories of the food species.

The last suggestion seems particularly important to me. Many people are now as much estranged from the lives of domestic plants and animals (except for flowers and dogs and cats) as they are from the lives of the wild ones. This is regrettable, for these domestic creatures are in diverse

ways attractive; there is much pleasure in knowing them. And farming, animal husbandry, horticulture, and gardening, at their best, are complex and comely arts; there is much pleasure in knowing them, too.

It follows that there is great *dis*pleasure in knowing about a food economy that degrades and abuses those arts and those plants and animals and the soil from which they come. For anyone who does know something of the modern history of food, eating away from home can be a chore. My own inclination is to eat seafood instead of red meat or poultry when I am traveling. Though I am by no means a vegetarian, I dislike the thought that some animal has been made miserable in order to feed me. If I am going to eat meat, I want it to be from an animal that has lived a pleasant, uncrowded life outdoors, on bountiful pasture, with good water nearby and trees for shade. And I am getting almost as fussy about food plants. I like to eat vegetables and fruits that I know have lived happily and healthily in good soil, not the products of the huge, bechemicaled factory-fields that I have seen, for example, in the Central Valley of California. The industrial farm is said to have been patterned on the factory production line. In practice, it looks more like a concentration camp.

The pleasure of eating should be an *extensive* pleasure, not that of the mere gourmet. People who know the garden in which their vegetables have grown and know that the garden is healthy will remember the beauty of the

growing plants, perhaps in the dewy first light of morning when gardens are at their best. Such a memory involves itself with the food and is one of the pleasures of eating. The knowledge of the good health of the garden relieves and frees and comforts the eater. The same goes for eating meat. The thought of the good pasture and of the calf contentedly grazing flavors the steak. Some, I know, will think it bloodthirsty or worse to eat a fellow creature you have known all its life. On the contrary, I think it means that you eat with understanding and with gratitude. A significant part of the pleasure of eating is in one's accurate consciousness of the lives and the world from which food comes. The pleasure of eating, then, may be the best available standard of our health. And this pleasure, I think, is pretty fully available to the urban consumer who will make the necessary effort.

I mentioned earlier the politics, aesthetics, and ethics of food. But to speak of the pleasure of eating is to go beyond those categories. Eating with the fullest pleasure—pleasure, that is, that does not depend on ignorance—is perhaps the profoundest enactment of our connection with the world. In this pleasure we experience and celebrate our dependence and our gratitude, for we are living from mystery, from creatures we did not make and powers we cannot comprehend. When I think of the meaning of food, I always remember these lines by the poet William Carlos Williams, which seem to me merely honest:

There is nothing to eat,
seek it where you will,
but the body of the Lord.
The blessed plants
and the sea, yield it
to the imagination
intact.

JANET BURROWAY

We Eat the Earth

Possessing what we still were unpossessed by,
Possessed by what we now no more possessed.
　　　　　　　　　　　—*Robert Frost*

For six years in the '60s I was tenant of an English garden.
Oh, my name was on the mortgage. I had come from as
far away as an Arizona childhood to teach English at the
University of Sussex, where my Belgian husband would
direct the Gardner Centre for the Arts. We had bought,
for what was then about thirty-four thousand dollars—
more than we could afford—a bleak brick box on two
acres of rolling land under the South Downs. The house
had big cube rooms smudged ocher with twenty years of
ash, and many mullioned windowpanes of which one
hundred eight were broken. But these windows looked

onto a garden that had been tended for thirty years by the man who had designed it so that no prospect would ever be free of flowers and it would yield food in every month. South, a gravel drive, a stand of bamboo and flowering cherry; west and north, lawns reaching to the ruin of a tennis court, lush rose beds and an orchard; and east to a greenhouse, more orchard, and a rectangle of about two-thirds of an acre "*laid to*" (as I learned to say) vegetables and fruit. You could see from this garden no other house, only fields cropped short by sheep and cows, sloping gently away or, beyond the road, rising to the crest of the Downs.

We could not really afford a gardener, but we could rent out the "staff flat" to graduate students, and the rent would pay for two and a half days a week of Mr. Ashley's time. Mr. Ashley said that he could find someone to hire him the other three days (we learned only gradually what an understatement this was), and so it was arranged. We told him to simplify in whatever way he needed to, in order to keep the garden in less than half the usual time. He said he would like a power hedge clipper and to eliminate one twenty-foot bed of dahlias. We said fine.

I was seven months pregnant when we moved in; we had a toddler as well as the two jobs. We set frantically to work with white paint on the ceilings and a sander on the crumbling-varnish floors. Mr. Ashley freewheeled down

the gravel in the early mornings in a peaked cap and a three-piece suit of hard tweed with a fob across the vest. He was white-haired, blue-eyed, trim, and soft-spoken. He never hurried but was seldom still. Invited inside, he demurred shyly. Invited to bring his wife to dinner, he declined embarrassed. He would not take a cup of tea. He called my husband "The Governor" and me "The Mrs."

In the third or fourth week, toward the end of September, he brought us a seed catalog and asked what we would like him to grow in the way of fruits and vegetables. We read through it, uneasy at our ignorance. We had no idea what could be grown in this soil or climate, or what would need too much care for two and a half days a week. After a while I took the catalog back outside and explained to Mr. Ashley that we had simply checked everything that, if he grew it, we would eat. "You decide whatever is convenient."

In an hour or so he was back at the back door. "Melons," he said hesitantly, "require daily care."

"Oh," I said. "Fine."

He fingered deliberately the pages of the catalog. "Otherwise that'll be all right."

And it was. In the greenhouse, tomatoes climbed and blazoned out of herbal beds; Belgian endive thickened its pallor inside upended terra-cotta pots. Cucumber vines tickled their way through seedling lettuce and early

radishes in the hothouse frames. Every year there were two sorts each of green beans, onions, spinach, peas (*petit* first and then English), cabbage, and carrots. There were garlic, scallions, turnips, cauliflower, beets, broccoli, brussels sprouts, kale, catnip, asparagus. We helped bag the potatoes and box the apples that lasted through the winter. Mr. Ashley braided the onions and the garlic. I went to school in the garden and I learned (ignorant child of Arizona!) that that black slash on a potato is the wound of a pitchfork. I learned how to put my foot on the edge of a spade, drive it straight so as not to hit the side of a leek, pull straight up, slice off the tops, and make vichyssoise (which the boys learned to call "swishy-swodge"). I canned peas. I put up a hundred pints of jam—strawberry, loganberry, gooseberry, red currant, and black currant. We bought a freezer, and I learned how to lay raspberries on a cookie sheet and bag them hard as marbles. I stewed and froze tomatoes. I scalloped and froze potatoes. We got a dog and cats, then rabbits and a goat. The dog and cats ate table scraps and the rabbits and goats digested the peels and husks of Mr. Ashley's bounty. I tried making elderberry wine (not much good). I made rhubarb tarts (superb). I dug and grated fresh horseradish. I dried mushrooms from the cow-rich field next door.

I have no vocabulary for those tastes. "Vine-ripened" is merest adspeak for a tomato's seeded juice, warm as the

palm of a hand. A carrot resists your tug, hugging the spring earth, and breaks sweet under grit. A bean snaps sharp on the teeth but asparagus yields with a soft *thock*. A potato just dug and boiled has the texture of hot snow. The half of the apple that hasn't rotted on the ground bites back with a tartness just this side of wine. Once a Belgian visitor to whom I served stew Gaston cried, "*On mange de la terre ici!*" and I thought, *We eat from the earth*. But the other translation feels also true: *we eat the earth*.

Not everything I learned had to do with food, of course. I learned how to stand white-knuckled at the sink letting the boys climb sixty feet into the horse-chestnut tree, and then how to thread the chestnuts so they could have conker wars. I learned how to gather a couple of hundred daffodils from the orchard in such a way that you couldn't tell I'd been there, how to cut roses on the diagonal an inch above the lowest five-leaf branch, how to balance a trug on my forearm and scrape the mud from my Wellingtons.

I never wanted to leave that garden, and remembering it makes the shape of the word "yearn" in my throat. From time to time I would dream I was walking down the lawn, which was full of fine ladies in cartwheel hats, trying to convince them that it had once been mine. I frequently performed little rituals of ownership, taking the children along the concrete paths that crossed the vegetable beds,

counting the rosebushes, smelling the apple trees, tug-
ging gingerly on the head of a raspberry but pinching
thumbnail-onto-finger through the stem of a gooseberry.
I became adept at seeing the camouflaged buds of peony
and laburnum in midwinter. I made a sweet infusion of the
first golden raspberry leaves. In difficult times—and there
were difficult times in the six years I was there—I sat at
the bottom of the vegetable plot with my back to the lo-
ganberry trellis, gazing at the Downs and chanting under
my breath, "I lift up mine eyes unto the hills."

But though I had registered for the long term, the
garden never belonged to me. For someone born into the
desert and the world of the typewriter, that plot of fecund
soil was akin to a computer: It could do far more than I
could take in or master. I surfed the legumes and the
roots, making demands to which they mysteriously com-
plied, but I was barely literate in their mysteries. Mr. Ash-
ley never to my knowledge tasted anything from "our"
rich patch—he had his own smaller garden. Every year we
entered his zucchini, his runner beans, his peonies and
irises in the Westmeston Flower Show, and (to his pride)
carried home his prizes. Even the three-toed carrot with
which Tim, seven, won the Weird Vegetable ribbon, was,
properly speaking, Mr. Ashley's deformity.

We struggled with the house, the children, the univer-
sity, a theater, each other. Mr. Ashley wheeled down the

gravel in every weather, sat in the wet in the shed sharpen-
ing his tools or braiding onions. When the weather broke
he was out again in his tweed vest and trousers, packing
straw under the berries (ignorant Arizonan!—so that's
where they got their names), tying up the runner beans,
bending little houses of chicken wire over the seedling peas
to thwart the field mice. Mr. Ashley was never absent. He
was never hurried. Nothing in the garden ever failed to
sprout or fruit. Once we wheedled him into a vacation and
he went with his wife to his brother's for a week—where,
Mrs. Ashley said, he sat and wrung his hands wanting to
get back to "our" raspberries and beets. I loved the garden
in bursts of energy and emotion, but I came to understand
that Mr. Ashley had the nature for a garden. I did not. I
was impetuous and rash. Invention was my virtue, and en-
thusiasm. Steady growing wants a steady guide, wants calm
and continuity, almost submission.

I had no obligation but to consume. Even so, the gar-
den's demands became heavier, or I became less capable of
meeting them. We were living in several ways beyond our
means. There were weekends when we sent visitors away
with armloads of squash and fennel and cabbage—but
could not afford to stand a round of drinks at the local pub.
Sometimes when we came home at midnight from the
Gardner Centre, weary with imminent production, Mr.
Ashley would have left word that the peas were ready, and

I would go into the garden with a flashlight to pick them, would stay up all night canning or freezing. How could I let them go to waste? When the production was over I would cook for cast parties, thick soups and mountains of sliced vegetables and berry parfaits. How could I not share such readily available wealth? I flung tops and stalks to the goat, who became unaccountably bad-tempered, and then threatening. I washed rivers of mud down the sink until the septic tank backed up.

In 1971 I left my husband, left England, left the garden. I took the boys, their toys, a suitcase apiece of essential clothes, and headed back to America with very little notion of what I was doing except that I had, in more ways than one, been living beyond my means. At Gatwick airport I folded my keys into an envelope addressed back to the Sussex house, and dropped the envelope in the post box. It was a chilly December dawn. When I crossed to the plane, a child on each hand, I had in my field of vision the black expanse of the tarmac, and suddenly superimposed on it the rows of turnip tops, the beans on their stakes, the rush of roses, the apple trees bending below the grassy hump of the Down. I was doing the right thing, I knew even then, and for that sick and stunning moment knew even then that I would never be done with grieving for the garden.

I still make stew Gaston and, peeling the potatoes for

it, hope to find the verifying black wound of somebody's pitchfork. I still make vichyssoise, from leeks I buy three at a time, a dollar apiece, at Publix. The boys, now thirty-one and thirty-three, still call it "swishy-swodge."

Watercress

During the week that my mother and I spent at Pancho's cabin, in Chile, in the '40s, her temper always changed when we went to the creek to get watercress. That dense squat plant, clinging to mud, weighed with some obscure sorrow. Nevertheless, it was too scary for a child to ask questions about the dark cloud the watercress cast over us.

We had met Pancho, jolly, roundish, and lushly mustachioed, at the *pensione* where we lived. A member of a family who owned a vast ranch in Chile belonged to the wealthy class, and a dentist was a member of the professional class; therefore we, as destitute refugees, had no reason to expect the friendship of such a personage, much

less the loan of his vacation cabin. We lived in a *pensione*
because we couldn't afford anything else. Pancho rented a
room to house toiletries, extra suits, ties, hankies, sports
outfits, and tuxedos. Astonishing, as my father owned one
pair of socks and one shirt, which could be washed only on
Saturday nights, to guarantee they would be dry on a
look-for-work day.

Pancho, who lived and worked downtown, would
come to his room-closet after work and leave freshly
dressed and combed and slapped with cologne, on his way
to see his girlfriend. Another perfumed member of the
well-to-do class, she lived in a mansion filled with dark
passages and darkly dressed aunts, three blocks away.
From there Pancho could make a quick run to our *pensione*
to dress up or down, if she had changed plans and maybe
wanted to go to the Opera House or perhaps to play ten-
nis. So Pancho the dentist was first my parents' fellow
rooming-house tenant, then their cheerful uncharging
dentist, and then a warm friend who loaned us his moun-
tain cabin.

Pancho's retreat was an adobe and tile-roofed piece of
heaven, perched up in the silent air of the Andes, in the
endless ranch owned by his family. At the back it had a
twig arbor with golden grapes, and two plum trees with
acidic bluish plums, which my mother cooked with sugar.
She concocted meals with the salami, condensed milk,
dried cod, sardines, the round tin of water crackers, cheese,

pasta, lentils, eggs, and the squash she had brought. Our main salad ingredient was watercress.

Everything in Pancho's cabin was sunny and sweet. We took daily walks and foraged for an occasional wild strawberry, blackberry, mushroom, mint, wild cherry or *pencas*, the juicy and delicious stalks of wild artichokes. Our forays were footloose, distracted, laced with my mother's hums, pieces of songs, talk, an occasional funny remark. But then, before dinner, as we picked the lush bunches of watercress that screamed "vitamins!" from the creek, my mother's silence was dense, and the evening cooled, suddenly darker over the rushing water.

Two or three days after we arrived, muddying the water as she swished the roots to clean them, my mother said in a tone of voice that gave me a lump, "You have no idea how much your *abuela*, grandmother, would love this watercress."

So, it was something about my *abuela*. I didn't remember her. When we had fled to France at the end of the Spanish civil war, we had become separated. Hitler was no friend of the Spanish refugees; when he started to invade his neighbors, it was time for Spanish Republicans to get out of Europe. The word went out that arrangements had been made for a cargo boat to take refugees to Latin America where, it was hoped, some country would grant us asylum.

On the appointed day for the boat's departure from

Le Havre, thousands, including my mother and father with me in tow, were there at dawn, hoping to be taken in. My *abuela* and my mother's family, however, were not. They never showed up. According to family versions gathered years later, the alarm clock of my mother's older brother, who was to go with his wife, child, parents, and younger brother to the ship, didn't work, or no one heard it, and they missed the boat, literally. They remained in France and worked at Nazi forced labor camps, where my mother's younger brother, at twenty-three, died from a broken back.

It was perfectly clear to me that while we were struggling in peaceful and beautiful Chile—the only country willing to take us—eating richly and abundantly, and now vacationing in a cocoon of mountains at a dentist's cabin, *la abuela* and the rest of the family, still caught in France at war, were subsisting on turnips, saccharin, chicory "coffee," and some rationed rice. Clearly, I was lucky; clearly, I should feel guilty. All this was tied to the watercress. But how, specifically? Did it have a link to some tragic event important to my mother? A happy event lost forever?

"You have no idea how much your *abuela* would love this watercress," my mother repeated the next day, bent over the creek. "If only we could send it to her." The look of the crisp watercress choked me. It barely moved, coolly, darkly, in the transparent stream, waving impossibilities: an impossibly vast ocean, failing alarm clocks, turnips and

saccharin, one war after another; impossibilities, but as real as the string from the window latch to the top corner of the armoire's door where our clothes dried; as a row of freshly pressed suits in a fragrant room; as the perpetually white peaks in warm weather at the top of the vertical walls of the Andes; as the noise of water over stones heading for the river, heading for the impossibly vast ocean.

At the end of the week we left Pancho's cabin, and nothing had been explained about the watercress.

Last week in my mother's kitchen in Madrid—where she returned, as did all her Spanish Republican friends, as soon as Franco died—I washed some watercress. The running water slid down the roundish leaves. For fifty-three years, they had held a dark, bittersweet childhood sorrow, vaguely linked to indebtedness, to helplessness, to the fearful unknown that was behind my mother's silence. I turned the water off and went to ask her about it.

She found it funny. "Maybe you can't be anguished all the time," she said, "so you pick one item to grieve over, and leave it at that." But, why watercress? Who knows? Maybe because it's so lush, so nutritious, so clean, so protected, so generous, so much like those who welcome and harbor refugees.

JOHN DUFRESNE

Nothing to Eat but Food:
Menu as Memoir

Never eat at a place called "Mom's."
—*Nelson Algren*

Throughout my childhood our family's evening meals were expeditious and purposeful, more reliable than imaginative. We were French Canadians, which meant we knew pork and maple syrup. My grandfather liked to eat salt pork, sautéed in a frying pan, or cold, right out of the fridge, with a schmear of horseradish, a side of string beans, and a bottle of Tadcaster ale. We were Catholics in a working-class neighborhood, so we did not expect or deserve joy at the supper table. Eating was a duty. Our table talk ran to imperatives and complaints: "You're not leaving the table until you've eaten every last bite of your supper." "Stop playing with your food." "Catsup's not as good as

ketchup." "My jaw hurts from chewing." "If you don't eat your vegetables, I'll sell you to the ragman." "This spinach is making me sick." Because our parents worked, Mom planned meals that we kids could easily execute. And once the menu was established, it did not vary for a dozen years. We didn't dine at our house; we ate the vernacular cuisine of Grafton Hill, a predominantly Irish enclave (you see how I'm trying to blame the Celts for this one— but think of it, corned beef and cabbage is their pride and joy!) in Worcester, Massachusetts. And this is what we ate.

MONDAY: *American Chop Suey.* Consider that there is no such dish as chop suey (*tsa tsui*—"a little of this and a little of that") in China. It's an American invention that's been around at least a hundred years. The Chun King company's canned version of this bastardized concoction, a gelatinous mass of unrecognizable vegetables and corn starch, covered with crispy, unsavory noodles, luscious as locusts, scares my sister Paula to this day. Now consider that in New England chop suey was considered too exotic, perhaps, or too unpatriotic, so a new dish, American chop suey, appeared. (Lin Yutang, who never ate chop suey in any version, said, "What is patriotism but the food of childhood?") This is what you might be served at a community bean supper if you were finally tired of beans. Traditionally, if we can use that word, American chop suey was made of ground beef, noodles, and tomato sauce. So

what it is then is a surrogate for a substitute. And our family took it all one step further by replacing the noodles with elbow macaroni and the sauce with canned tomato soup. Brown the beef, boil the macaroni, drain into a bowl, pour in the soup, and mix.

Call it the cuisine of simulation. We embraced replacement foods. We drank Kool-Aid instead of juice. Oleo was cheaper than butter, and so the kids ate that while Dad hoarded his Land O Lakes. We asked him, "Who do you trust, chemists or farmers?" "You guys can't tell the difference anyway," he said. We didn't eat pizza, we ate mock pizza—a rasher of bacon, a slice of tomato, and a slice of American cheese (orange preferred, yellow acceptable) on an English muffin. Broiled. My mother made what she always called ham salad for sandwiches, but the ham was ground bologna, mixed with pickles and mayo. We even used maple extract to make ersatz maple syrup. And we learned that milk could taste bad if it was powdered.

Even though we got our four quarts of cream-line milk delivered three times a week from Lundgren & Jonaitis Dairy (*You can whip our cream, but you can't beat our milk!*), it was never enough. (We also had bread delivered by the Cushman Bread man, but he was retained because of the coffee cakes and pastries and because my aunts thought he was cute.) Mom bought the powdered stuff (Carnation,

Sanalac) and mixed gallon batches of it at a time. But it was blue and had laundry-detergentlike crystals floating on the surface and a strangely medicinal taste, so she took to mixing half powdered and half real milk, which only succeeded in defiling the genuine article. It was during this bleak and frugal period, I remember, that Mom thought to serve blood sausage—*boudin*, an excrementally foul, cordovan-colored bladder of pig's blood, suet, bread crumbs, and oatmeal—and tried to pass it off as a savory ethnic delicacy. No wonder I drank Hershey's chocolate syrup right out of the can.

TUESDAY: *Meat Loaf.* My mother made her loaf with ground beef, bread crumbs, water, tomato soup (not sauce), with perhaps a dab of Worcestershire, but no onions. The mixture was firmly shaped in a baking pan on Monday night, covered with wax paper, and stored in the fridge. When cooked, sliced, and served the loaf was slightly pulpy and decidedly gray on the inside, with a crumbly brown crust. Food was not prepared with enticement or cleverness in mind. Our gastronomic philosophy was, *Look, you eat or you die, so let's just get it over with and get on with living.* Speed was essential in the cooking and in the eating. We never had dessert during the week, seldom had salad. One-course meals were the rule. Speedily eaten and speedily constructed. We were not ashamed.

The notion of simplicity and haste extended to school lunches, which we carried in brown bags. We each made our own lunch the night before, and lunch was never anything other than a single sandwich. In my case, two slices of Nissen's enriched white bread, oleo on one, bright yellow mustard on the other, and a slice of bologna between them. I didn't even cut the sandwich in half. Lunch was as thin as a notebook and as crass as Muzak.

With Tuesday's meat loaf we had potatoes, peeled, quartered, and boiled. And boiled. Boiled until they were dry, friable, insipid. They sat on the plate, shoulders hunched, defeated and frightening in their sallowness. We had to salt them, pepper them, margarine them just to raise a molecule of taste.

WEDNESDAY: *Anything-Can-Happen Day.* On Wednesday we experimented—within reason—with what I suppose we could call *"vulgar cuisine,"* in that it was common, somewhat deficient in taste, and coarse: the food of the masses—those estranged from their ethnic heritage, at any rate. We might have shepherd's pie, which we called *"paté de chinois"* for some reason. Our shepherds, however, herded beef, not sheep. Ground beef was again the main ingredient. Beef, mashed potatoes, corn. Or we might try something more exotic like chicken à la king—diced chicken, cream of mushroom soup, hold the pimientos. Or beef stew. More often than not we ate meat—a roast—

with a vegetable, and boiled potatoes. Mom would call from work at four and tell Paula or Dee Dee to put the roast in the oven at 350 degrees, boil six potatoes, open two cans of green beans, and simmer them. The idea of fresh vegetables occurred to us only in the summer when the native corn was harvested, the sweetest, tenderest, most delicious corn around, I might add, even if boiled for thirty minutes. The South built a culture around vegetables: sweet potato casserole, collards, hoppin' John, grits. We, however, made do with cans of waxed beans or beets or grayish, mushy green peas. On Wednesdays the dog ate well. Shep sat under the table once our parents left to watch the news. He'd eat anything.

Ours was discomfort food. Our motto: Let no food offend with assertive taste. Which may be why I have become addicted to hot and spicy foods, why I would drive, and have driven, across the country for a good meal. I'm still not sophisticated about food—how could I be?—but I know that I can be cheered and restored by the straightforward foods I crave: by the chili, say, at La Posta in Mesilla, New Mexico, or by the barbecued mutton and ribs at Sam's in Austin, or by the salty, sweet oysters fresh from the Gulf at the Acme Oyster House in New Orleans.

THURSDAY: *Spaghetti and Meatballs.* First of all, we drew distinctions among spaghetti, macaroni, and pasta

that Italians did not. Macaroni meant elbow macaroni as used in the American chop suey or served with butter and ketchup. (This is not something I'm proud of, but confession is good for the soul: I still eat macaroni with butter and ketchup. I love it, but I don't indulge when anyone else is in the apartment. And while we're on the subject, I sometimes steal a box of my son's Kraft macaroni and cheese and add a lot of curry.) Thin spaghetti was used in the Thursday-night meatball feast. Pasta was everything else, and we never ate it. Not ziti, not shells, not pastina, not fettucine, not cavatelli, none of it. Egg noodles didn't end in a vowel and so could not be pasta. And yes, we did eat Franco-American spaghetti, but only for lunch.

My mother's meatballs were made with ground beef and ground pork. She made a wonderful sauce, uncharacteristically tangy, spicy, garlicky, and thick, better than all my Italian friends' moms'. And she added sweet Italian sausage to the mix. We might even have fresh bread from D'Amico's Market instead of the spongy stuff we were used to. So Thursday was easily the best meal of the week, but it was also the most tense. It was Dad's payday, and that always meant a discussion about where the rest of the money went, and how am I supposed to feed four kids on this and pay the bills, and so on. Dad would hand Mom the cash from his back pocket, and she'd ask him for the pay stub that he had always managed to lose. We did not

savor our food on Thursday; we scarfed it. We swallowed quickly and went outside to play hide-and-seek in the street or stickball in the schoolyard.

FRIDAY: *Tuna Noodle Casserole*. Catholics didn't eat meat on Friday in those days, and so we were saved from another version of ground beef. We had tuna noodle casserole, a blend of egg noodles, peas, tuna, and mushroom soup, baked and covered with State Line potato chips. Occasionally, Mom would inexplicably and daringly crumble Ritz crackers on top in lieu of potato chips. We were rattled. But since we did crumble Ritz crackers on our soup, we figured it was all right. Just don't make a habit of it. Potato chips in a meal, you realize, was like sneaking in another snack.

Worcester was filled with take-out fish-and-chips joints that catered to abstaining Catholics and opened only on Fridays. We had several in our neighborhood. Here you could get fried clams (with the bellies, of course; the strips didn't exist then, and no New Englander would ever eat one anyway, the bellies being the whole point of fried or steamed clams), fried scallops, and of course, fish and chips. So occasionally we might get take-out orders. But we seldom ate supper at a restaurant, and when we did it was always Messiers, a diner that specialized in seafood. It's where we went after First Communions and graduations, Mother's Day, that sort of thing.

Worcester, by the way, gave the world the diner. Sure, there had been lunch carts earlier in Providence and Springfield, but Sam Jones opened the first sit-down mobile cart at the corner of Main and Front Streets in 1884. And Worcester's where native T. H. Buckley opened his New England Night Lunch Wagon Company to manufacture lunch carts. There followed the Worcester Lunch Car and Carriage Manufacturing Company, J. J. Hennigan, and other builders of diners, and the rest is pop culture history. The Miss Worcester Diner is the oldest diner in the country, and it's still open.

SATURDAY *Frankfurts and Beans.* I think it was mandatory in Worcester that every family had franks and beans on Saturday night. Kayem or Maple Leaf hot dogs were the brands of choice. B&M molasses baked beans were local favorites although we went for the tomato-based Campbell's, no surprise there. The only thing I knew about molasses in those days was that we always had a half-empty bottle of Brer Rabbit molasses in the back of the fridge by the can of bacon fat and the bottle of Karo syrup. And since we never used it, it probably wasn't bland enough.

The hot dogs were boiled until they split. The beans warmed on the stove. We had canned brown bread with the meal. Ketchup, yellow mustard, sweet pickle relish. And maybe it would be snowing outside and we'd get to stay up late and watch scary movies and maybe get to eat

TV Time popcorn and drink some tonic. The world was magnificent on Saturday nights.

SUNDAY: *Pot Roast.* Dinner is supper in the afternoon, and it only happens on Sunday. We spent every Sunday after Mass at my grandparents' apartment. Our large extended family (my grandfather being one of nineteen children) managed to sit down for a dinner of pot roast, brown potatoes roasted with the drippings, and vegetables. The wonderful part of Sunday was that we always had dessert. My grandmother made three pies every week: chocolate cream, apple (made with Macouns or Baldwins), and blueberry. My job was to stand on a stool and whip the cream with the eggbeater. Three hundred cranks. If a new can of coffee was needed, I could open it with the key, unwind the ribbon of razor-sharp tin, hear the hiss of expelled air, and inhale the aroma of fresh coffee, one of my favorites, along with baking bread, frying garlic, vanilla, and gasoline.

We saved the coffee cans for my grandfather's worms. Pepere raised worms in the cellar in a large tub by the coal bin. He fed them newsprint—cellulose the attraction, I guess. When we went fishing we scooped up a couple of dozen crawlers in our Maxwell House can and headed to the lake. (Worms, by the way are 72 percent protein and only 1 percent fat. The Chinese have a soup called *tio in tin tun,* which calls for earthworms. You slit them open

and wash them to remove the soil. Simmer them in water until the broth is reduced by half. Serve warm.) In winter we ice-fished with shiners. Pepere kept the shiners alive in the bathtub on the night before our expeditions.

We'd leave Memere and Pepere's house late in the afternoon and swing by Water Street, the old Jewish quarter of town, and in the days of blue laws, the only place where businesses were open on Sunday. Water Street was paved with cobblestones, and I loved the sound of tires fluttering over the stones. I loved the yeasty smells from the bakeries, the bustle of shoppers. We'd buy bulkies and cream cheese and head to my father's parents' house for a kind of evening brunch with all the paternal relatives. Bulkies, by the way, are sandwich buns—hard rolls with or without poppy seeds, great with cold cuts, cream cheese, or simply grilled with butter. (Beware: There are nine hundred thousand poppy seeds in a pound, and they *will* get stuck between your teeth.) We called hard rolls "bulkies," subs "grinders," soda "tonic," ice cream cups "Hoodsies," sprinkles "jimmies," milk shakes "frappes" (or "cabinets"), a small store with a lunch counter a "spa," we took the -er off hamburg*er* and frankfurt*er*, we called catfish "horn pout," poached eggs "dropped eggs," and we drank our water from a "bubbler."

So the adults ate the bulkies and cream cheese and the kids sat at the metal fold-out table and ate cereal with milk and sugar directly from the little boxes. I sat below the

black-cat clock, its eyes and tail moving side to side. I never got the cereal I wanted. I only liked Wheaties, but I could tolerate Rice Krispies. What I'd end up with was Sugar Pops, or Raisin Bran, or Kix, or something equally dreadful. Why was this happening to me? Isn't there a can of fruit cocktail around? Some yellow cling peaches in heavy syrup? Can somebody fry me some bologna? A piece of bread with butter and ketchup? Pretty soon Ed Sullivan would come on the TV, and I'd realize that once again I hadn't done a lick of homework over the weekend and I was doomed. Sister would be taking the ruler to the backs of my lazy hands. Me, an altar boy, in disgrace once again.

I became an altar boy so that I could be alone. I was as spiritually devout as any of my friends, I suppose, more so probably, since I was terrified of hell and, being a young hypochondriac, always certain I was near death. I wanted in on the mystery of the Mass, the Latin, the incense, the transubstantiation. But what I enjoyed most about all this was my long, solitary walks those dark mornings to St. Stephen's Church. Better even in winter, in the snow. A little bit of martyrdom involved. Best on Saturdays. No traffic. No school. Quiet. And when six o'clock Mass let out, I took off my cassock and surplice, the taste of the Host still on my palate, carried the cruets, empty of water and wine, back to the rectory, and crossed the street to Tony's Spa. I sat at the counter by myself, ordered a

grilled corn muffin and a chocolate milk. Fifteen cents. I'd watch the snow fall on Grafton Street through Tony's frosted plateglass window, think about the day ahead, about basketball later at the junior high gym. And then maybe candlepin bowling or sledding or a walk to the library and then to my grandmother's for Toll House cookies by the stove. A good book, a warm room, the comfort of chocolate and crumb.

Spaghetti

In the den of our old house in Springfield, I remember an ancient black Naugahyde reclining chair, taped and tattered, the works so broken it wouldn't recline anymore; a fraying oval of Oriental carpet around whose whorls and arabesques I pushed Matchbox cars encrusted from the dirt pile out back; an ominous couch covered in green, itchy fabric, flanked by two rather funereal lamps; and in the far corner beside the window always kept shuttered, a huge dusty television with a very small screen, outdated even then. This last item, of German manufacture—a Telefunken, I think—had been acquired by my parents in occupied Vienna in the '50s. The cabinetry was beautiful,

inlaid wood and marquetry, but the black-and-white pic-
ture was always too bright or too dark, the sound inter-
mittent at best.

One evening in the early '60s—I was no more than
two or three—I sat cross-legged on the carpet, my face
tipped up toward the glowing screen. A slow countdown
vibrated from the speakers and then a silver projectile—
probably one of the Mercury rockets—blasted into the
sky above Cape Canavarel, trailing smoke like white feath-
ers. I don't know now why I sat in the den alone watching
this monumental event: the rest of the family was in the
kitchen, just settling down to dinner. But moments after
the rocket passed the low clouds and became a silver glint
in the gray sky of the television, my mother called me to
the table. The spaghetti was ready.

I tottered across the living room into the kitchen's
yellow light just as my father lifted the long strands of
wheat-colored spaghetti from the steel pot. Another pot
contained thick, fragrant red sauce swimming with meat-
balls large as my fist. Plates were passed across the
turquoise Formica counter and returned heaping to the
white tablecloth. Rich, red sauce covered every plate ex-
cept for mine and my mother's. She ate her spaghetti
plain, with salt and butter, a perversity that bears some ex-
plaining. I was too young to know better. The steely side
of the pot of spaghetti on the stove showed the same sil-

ver glint of the rocket on its way into space as my mother
bowed her head for the blessing.

This is probably my first memory.

My parents made their strange bargain in the late 1940s in
Washington, D.C., in the exuberant days just after the
war. The bargain itself was of the usual sort: that they
would marry, raise children, make a life together. It was
only strange because they had nothing in common. Not
blood, perspective, culture, cuisine. The hardest part of
the bargain encompassed the understanding that my fa-
ther would abandon his culture as an ethnic Italian Amer-
ican to become an unhyphenated American in what was
then the American century, and that my mother would
leave her people behind to facilitate this transformation.

He was short, fond of dancing, good food, wine; a
solid, first-generation Italian from a small coal-mining
town just outside of Pittsburgh. She was tall, American,
grave, dignified, never danced, and was partial to plain
roast beef, strong opinions, and nights at home; an eccen-
tric white Anglo-Saxon Catholic from a line of eccentric
white Anglo-Saxon Catholics who dated their presence on
these shores back to 1634. Her ancestors had come over on
the *Arc* and *Dove*, two famous ships that brought the first
and last English Catholic settlers across the Atlantic to es-
tablish the colony that later became the state of Maryland.

Of course, my mother's parents were opposed to her marriage from the beginning. They would not tolerate their daughter marrying a foreigner, they said, and threatened to disown her if she did. Pointing out that my father was a Pennsylvanian who had served honorably in the U.S. Army during the war did nothing to sway their resolve. At twenty-five my mother still lived with her parents, on the dormer floor of a well-kept, spacious Victorian house on Kanawah Street in northwest Washington. There were some stiff, ugly scenes, then she packed her things secretly one night in November 1946 and took a Greyhound bus to Pennsylvania with the remains of her savings hidden in a white leather cosmetics bag in her suitcase.

Even at its most prosperous, there was something baroque and foreboding about my father's hometown, folded into the hills above the brown sluice of the Allegheny River. Now it is abandoned, empty, a maze of broken factories and rusting corrugated iron, as if in fulfillment of an evil promise. But in those days the air above its row houses and steep streets hung thick with the fires of the great smelters, and trucks full of plate steel roared up and down the highway through town; Pittsburgh blossomed, a black smudge of coal smoke on the horizon.

My mother stayed at the YWCA on Main Street downtown near the Alhambra movie theater, now closed, while last preparations went forward with the inevitability of an execution. My father's mother and his sisters cooked

for three days straight for the wedding feast. His uncle, a wizened little Italian man who rarely spoke, dug up the last precious homemade wine laid in the ground during Prohibition; wine made from secret black grapes grown somewhere in the hills overlooking the town.

The wedding reception took place in the Knights of Columbus hall across from the Catholic church on a rainy afternoon. The rain, full of coal soot, spotted my mother's white satin dress. Friends of my father still talk about the food: A mighty spread of antipasti covered three trestle tables; five more tables sagged beneath the weight of fifteen different kinds of pasta—including baked ziti, cannelloni, stuffed shells, lasagna; even *timpano*, which is a sort of pie of pasta, cheese, ham, onions, and sweetbreads— baked suckling pig Calabrian-style, chicken cacciatore, a half-dozen rich desserts. My mother wouldn't touch a bite. She didn't like Italian food. Italian food was for Italians. It was as simple as that. And she would have no wine. She didn't drink, either.

I can imagine my Italian relatives sadly shaking their heads. My Italian grandfather and grandmother, both of whom died long before I was born, must have been disappointed. I imagine them like Indians in a grade-B Western, puzzled over the mysterious ways of white people. What sort of creature could fail to be tempted by so much good food? And I can see her there, my mother, resplendent in her spotted white satin, superior, dignified, not eating, not

drinking. She is like Persephone in Hades, pale as an apparition as the *tarantella* plays, as the feast whirls around her in all its vulgar color. Wine flows and my cousins cram ziti into their mouths, the *timpano* is cut, releasing a cloud of aromatic steam—but she is dreaming of overdone Anglo-Saxon pot roast and Jell-O molds, of limp string beans and parsleyed potatoes, of unsauced chicken, of dry turkey on a bed of plain iceberg lettuce.

Her revenge for this single evening of Italian culinary excess was a slow and subtle torment that lasted through forty-five years of married life: Six days a week, she inflicted the food she had dreamed of the night of her wedding on her husband and family. Only on Sunday were we allowed a respite from the bland English fare of her forefathers. On that day she would condescend to make spaghetti from the recipe handed down in my father's family. But this, too, as it turned out, was part of her revenge—the pasta on her plate, gleaming, unadorned, bare of sauce, reproached us with every swallow.

My Italian Aunt Philomena in her retirement kept a little house in St. Petersburg, Florida, where we spent summer vacation once or twice during the turbulent years between the Kennedy assassination and Kent State. There, as traveller palms swayed outside the aluminum frame window, she patiently taught my mother how to make the sauce. The preparation had a ritualistic quality that col-

ored Sundays in my youth every bit as much as Mass: The meatballs were started in the morning and lowered into the sauce to cook all day. By afternoon the fragrance of simmering meat, tomatoes, and spices filled our tepid suburban bungalow as piazzas in towns in Italy are full of golden light in the hour before the sun goes down. The fragrance of the sauce cooking was no mere odor; it was family history in a smell.

My Italian grandfather, a tough-as-nails, scrupulously honest Calabrian, was born in the '70s of the last century, barely ten years after Garibaldi united the peninsula for the first time since the collapse of the Roman Empire. A moderately prosperous man by the dusty standards of his country, my grandfather owned two small olive farms near Catanzaro, three or four mules, a wine press. But he abandoned everything and joined the great migration to America in the early 1900s for reasons still obscure, which probably had everything to do with a Mafia vendetta.

Later, in Pennsylvania, he got a job on a crew that cleaned up wrecks for the railroad, worked his way up to foreman, fathered fourteen children, and at the end of his life became known as something of a storyteller. Old Italian men from the neighborhood would come over, sample his homemade wine and stuffed peppers, and listen to him tell the one about the fisherman who caught a fish that

gave him three wishes, or the one about the man who had ears so big that he could hear things happening on the other side of the earth.

When my grandfather died in the early '50s, a long black limousine pulled up graveside, and a dignified man in an expensive suit—the local Mafia Don—stepped out and approached the family. Two thugs followed along behind, carrying large black wreaths. The Don greeted my father with an old-world bow and asked permission to lay the wreaths on the coffin. "We respected your father," he explained. "He wouldn't have anything to do with us. He was an honest man."

They laid the wreaths, got back into the car, and drove away.

The sauce for our spaghetti is not difficult to master. My aunt's other recipes—her frittatas, stuffed pork, squid in its own ink, rigatoni and chicken livers—have been lost. The sauce recipe was passed on to my mother as a young bride, as a sort of sacred responsibility. After a hostile if careful custodianship, she passed it on to me. In college in the late '70s and early '80s, my reputation as an excellent cook and sensitive guy was based on my ability to make a decent spaghetti and meatballs. Coeds at Virginia those days seemed to be impressed by this; I can remember several meals that paved the way down the hall to the bedroom.

Now, my wife knows the truth. Spaghetti is the only dish in my repertoire. I make it on Sundays for the family and she cooks the other days of the week. She is a good cook, she loves food, and her palate is mercifully more sophisticated than my mother's.

I haven't been exactly fair to the English, here. As everyone knows, they are not famous for their cooking. The great achievements of the English lie elsewhere. Obviously there is a certain imperial virtue in bland food. One is not long at the table over a meal of boiled steak and kidney pie, or pork chops done like shoe leather; one is instead quickly out into the world, civilizing savages, building bridges across cataracts, deciphering tomb inscriptions, irrigating deserts, and finding the cure for malaria. The English have always been a restless race, unhappy on their rainy isle and unhappy away from it—a trait passed down like cancer in my mother's family.

One of my great-great-grandfathers on the maternal side ran away from Charlotte's Hall Military Academy at the age of fifteen in 1862 to join the Confederacy and was dragged home from the front by his mother. Another ran off to live with the Plains Indians and was never heard of again. Still another took ship for the Amazon to hunt for emeralds, and his fate, too, is unknown. Perhaps they were running from the bland food at home, or perhaps something else drove them on, simmering in their blood like

meatballs in a sauce: a taste for the exotic that can be de-
tected in—for example—the late works of J. M. W. Turner,
that most English of painters.

I do not remember when I first began taking my spaghetti
with sauce and meatballs; no doubt it represented a rebel-
lion from which my mother never quite recovered. I do re-
member the first time I attempted the sauce in college, and
called my mother for the recipe. There was a certain irony
mixed with the ingredients as she drawled them out to me
over the phone, a tacit admission of defeat. Recipes are
strange things. The power of great food resides in the fact
that, like music, its meaning is beyond words.

According to my father, my Italian grandmother,
when cooking in the kitchen with her older sister, spoke a
language that was not Italian, that was a private language
known and shared between the two of them. Later he
guessed it was probably a vestigial Albanian dialect. There
had been a migration of Albanians to the southern parts of
Italy during the fourteenth century, following the Turkish
invasion of the Balkans; an ancient Albanian college ex-
isted in Calabria until the last years of the nineteenth cen-
tury. I imagine my grandmother and her sister speaking
softly in this forgotten tongue as they labored over the
sauce for spaghetti and meatballs later handed down to
me; an artifact from a hard, beautiful landscape—arid,

suspended between dry yellow hills and deep blue water—
that will never be my own.

All artists, I think, suffer from a mild form of synes-
thesia, that metaphoric condition where a taste or a smell
or a sound can call up the immediate image of something
utterly different—the taste of roast beef, say, conjuring a
vision of marble arches or the inside of a carburetor. A
few weeks ago a friend gave me a recording of Argentine
tangos from the 1920s and 1930s performed by Carlos
Gardel, known to everyone south of the Equator as the
undisputed "King of the Tango." When I sat down and lis-
tened to the creaky, passionate music, my mouth immedi-
ately recalled the complex richness and spice of the family
spaghetti sauce, and I knew for the first time why my
mother never liked the stuff. It was the same reason she
never liked to dance.

Girardi's spaghetti and meatballs, modernized for convenience

Ingredients

For the meatballs: one-half pound of Italian sausage meat,
mild; one-half pound of lean ground beef; a raw egg; one
cup of finely diced red onion; four pieces of stale sourdough
bread, cubed; one-half cup of red wine; one teaspoon of
dried oregano; one-half teaspoon of powdered garlic.

For the sauce: one large can of whole, peeled tomatoes; one cup of red wine; one large red onion, quartered; one heaping tablespoon each of dried oregano, basil, thyme; one level teaspoon of powdered garlic; one level teaspoon of sugar; hot red pepper to taste; one-half cup of olive oil; one-half pound of fresh mushrooms, sliced, a couple of bay leaves.

Directions

For the meatballs: Beat egg; soak bread cubes in red wine. Combine ground beef, sausage meat, beaten egg, bread cubes, spices, onions; mix thoroughly and form into roughly ten meatballs. Fry meatballs in olive oil until brown and firm.

For the sauce: Place quartered onion in blender; dump can of tomatoes on top. Add spices, olive oil, wine. Blend on high until absolutely pureed. Pour sauce into large pot; add browned meatballs and mushrooms. Bring to a boil briefly, then simmer, stirring regularly for at least one hour—but the longer the better. Remove the bay leaves; serve with salad, garlic bread, and a dash of history.

JESSICA B. HARRIS

In a Leaf
of Collard, Green

With apologies to Langston Hughes

Many years ago, when I was teaching one of my first English courses, I came across *Ask Your Mama*, a collection of poems by Langston Hughes. In one, the recurring image, "in a leaf of collard, green," came back to haunt me. I, too, have been marked by the large, purplish-tinged leaves that are, along with okra and watermelon, the African Americans' culinary mark of Cain. Collard greens have followed me all of my life and remain something I don't want to live without. They have punctuated my life, perfuming each phase with their pungent aroma.

One of my earliest memories is of my paternal grandmother. I see her in my mind's eye, tall and African-regal.

Her hair is parted neatly into the four braids she always wore. Her faded housedress with its lacy collar is neatly pressed and her large feet are shod in old-lady shoes with the toes cut out on either side. We're outside in the small garden plot she cultivated behind the projects in Jamaica, Queens. She is bent almost double weeding and arranging, tending each plant as though it were one of the many neighborhood children who called her Mama Harris and flocked around her. The garden plot is small but she somehow manages to keep her southern roots alive, growing black-eyed peas, peanuts, and the largest rosettes of leafy green that are collards in the shade of the Long Island Railroad tracks. I must have been very small indeed as I remember looking up at the trains as they went by and wondering where they went and what kind of people rode them, surprisingly rural thoughts for an urban child of the 1950s.

I liked all of the foods Grandma Harris cooked; she wasn't a great cook, but she excelled at southern classics like beaten biscuits. Her southern tastes were different from the more European dishes that my Pratt-educated mother placed on our dinner table at home. While my mother's food marked my universe, everyone in the family acknowledged that Grandma Harris could "put a hurtin' on some greens."

After the first frost hit them, Grandma and I would gather the greens and take them upstairs to her third floor

apartment. There, she'd fill the deep porcelain sink in her tiny kitchen with cold water and soak the leaves. Then with deft movements of her gnarled brown hands, it was strip and tear, discarding ones that were blemished or not up to her standards. Finally she'd place them in a large pot with a piece of "streak of lean/streak of fat" and onto the four-burner stove on which she also made lye soap. Grandma's tastes of her southern home marked me for life.

My taste for the leafy greens followed me when I left my parents' house and headed off to college. Bryn Mawr, if you please. There's no place in the world where you were less likely to find collard greens than in the Bryn Mawr of the mid 1960s. I don't know how the six other black coeds in my class coped, but Grandma took care of my greens jones. I could count on the care packages I would receive. Neatly wrapped brown-paper parcels arrived regularly, addressed in the carefully rounded hand of one who had learned how to write late in life and still delighted in the formation of the letters. Inside were jars of greens I could open and enjoy. Little did I know that Grandma's care packages were doing double duty—feeding not only my stomach, but gently and quietly reminding me of my blackness amidst the groves of ivy and keeping me grounded in my heritage and myself.

Grandma's reach didn't extend to Paris, where I spent my junior year; I was on my own. My care packages couldn't survive the rigors of transatlantic travel. I slowly

forgot about them and their importance in my life. When Grandma Harris died, the Easter of that year, I was too saddened by the loss and too involved with the wonders of the continent to realize that the torch had been passed. I was not so involved that I didn't discover other leaves in the tiny shops of the rue Mouffetard: African greens with mysterious names, leaves from the Caribbean that looked like large elephant ears, and more. Over the years I would sample these other greens in the sauces and soups, stews and salads.

It was only after years of sampling, that one day in an open market in Abidjan, as I watched a woman prepare a sauce *feuilles*, I made the connection with Grandma Harris and her greens. There was something about the way the woman stripped the greens, her hands working automatically from years of experience, moving with a rhythm they had learned from some unknown ancestor: picking, sorting, stripping, tearing. The penny dropped. Our greens were the same as their greens. Not only were Grandma Harris's greens southern; their manner of preparation extended back over time and across an ocean.

Since that culinary epiphany in the Cocody market under the hot sun, I've cooked greens on four continents and am always looking for new ways to prepare the collards and other leaves that have become one of my culinary hallmarks. There's a Zenlike meditative quality to preparing greens. As you stand facing the sink or the

basin, the mind floats off to other thoughts and the hands take over: washing, picking, rinsing, stripping, rinsing, and tearing.

Although I've had lots of experience with the process, I'm still not the mistress of greens in my home. Each year when I give my New Year's open house and prepare a traditional Black American menu with greens as one of the centerpiece dishes, I make the southern succotash of okra, corn, tomatoes, and hot chili; I roast the huge fresh pork with cracklings; I cook the black-eyed peas and rice. My mother makes the greens. I wouldn't have it any other way.

Chinese Spareribs

My sister and I stand shoulder to shoulder in the designer kitchen of her West County home. A friendly argument ensues. I want another five cloves of garlic. She insists that we passed the garlic threshold a half a head ago and is set on "diluting" the batter with a handful of flour. We are engaged in a futile attempt to re-create my father's recipe for Chinese spareribs and feel ourselves getting closer, much the way a researcher might feel honing in on the gene that causes pleasure. We know we're in the neighborhood, we're damn close, in fact. But something's off. Something's not quite right. In fact, we're "pretending" close: we've gotten our ribs to the point where, if we play

pretend and then accompany that pretense with a couple of glasses of wine, we can fool ourselves into believing that we are back in our house on St. Gabriel Court, and that it's New Year's Day, around four in the afternoon, and we've just had placed on the table before us, in those two bizarrely hourglass-shaped black melmac serving bowls that our father favored, heaping glistening mounds of Daddy's ribs.

Close—pretend close, even—but no cigar.

Tender, succulent, pungent, rich. How to describe Chinese spareribs. Let's begin by making perfectly clear what they are not. They are not those dryish, red-tinted things that appear on the appetizer menu of every hole-in-the-wall Chinese joint in America. Don't get me wrong, I've chomped down my fair share of those babies over the years, believe me. (Though I've always been troubled by that crimson rind. Where exactly does that come from? Are we sure this is something we should be eating?)

Chinese spareribs also have nothing to do with barbecued spareribs—a dish, I tell you with a mixture of pride and envy, that my sister has not only mastered but bested my father on. Damn her, I still chauvinistically maintain that ribs are a guy thing, but my sister can wield her sauce mop with the best of the boys. It's the sauce that's the secret, of course, though not with my father's Chinese spareribs. They don't have sauce: They have breading!

For those not in the know, it is breading in its many

exquisite forms that lies at the heart of much of the fine cuisine of the world. My father coated his dish with a garlicky crust, and between us, with any number of advanced degrees and a whole repertoire of our own killer crusts, what my sister and I cannot figure out is what it was that that man put in the bowl to make those ribs so damn tasty. Was it some secret brand of soy sauce? Did he used plain sugar or brown sugar? (Or was there, indeed, any sugar in there at all?) Or perhaps we have taken the wrong tack entirely. Maybe the secret is the grease. Maybe it is that you have to heat it to just the right temperature, or, more likely, maybe it's the combination of whatever flavors came out of his treasured grease canister that sat there at the back of the stove for as long as I can remember. Underneath the lid it contained a special sieve for filtering out the grit and gravel that frying a rasher of bacon always produced. Modern black folks that we are, neither my sister nor I would be so crass as to actually have a can of grease parked on our range. How, after all, would one explain such a low-class object when the folks from the office drop by for cocktails? (At least my parents had an actual kitchen implement invented for this purpose. A lot of you, and *you know who you are*, just have that old Crisco can sitting there for all to see.) Alas, progress: My sister and I try to make do with our health-conscious vegetable oils. Who are we kidding? What we're doing, after all, is

frying pork ribs! The healthy-diet police have orders to shoot us on sight. And we don't even have the stupid recipe right.

We sit there with our family and pick politely at our ribs and rice, kicking ourselves for not paying attention. Between us we have seen this meal prepared hundreds of times. Our facsimile merely shadows what we all remember.

Adolescents are more or less required by statute not to pay much attention to anything that their parents say or do. But putting down this lost treasure to pubescent alienation is too simplistic. In fact, like most fine chefs, my father guarded his culinary secrets like the treasure they were. We certainly could have and should have asked how he did it—he would have liked that. But while he might have gladly talked us through the process, letting us stand right next to him and watch, he would have no more disclosed the mystery ingredient or technique or time or temperature or whatever in God's name made his special dinner so . . . special than he would have sold his family down the river.

The Hayneses were blessed with a family where food was important and communal, the center of our home life, really. Until the general chaos of teenage life pulled us in a thousand directions, my mother cooked a full meal for dinner five nights a week. Having mastered Swiss steak,

pot roast, chicken and dumplings, and chili, Mama could best be called a classic, *Betty Crocker's Cookbook*–trained mid-South chef. What the savvy marketers and ethnographers now call "soul" food, I knew as just the regular side dishes sprinkled throughout the week. Macaroni and cheese (which has nothing to do with the stuff that comes in the box, and, importantly, involves eggy/cheesy lumps and plenty of crunchy dark-brown crust), greens, neckbones, candied yams, black-eyed peas and rice, etc.; this was mundane fare at our house.

Mother had her on-days and her off-days in the kitchen. When she was on, every last piece of fried chicken (including the neck!) would disappear from the platter where it rested upon a stack of paper towels transparent with the same bacon fat and Crisco my father used for his spareribs. Mama had an iron skillet that she used to sizzle them bad boys to a golden brown. Every grain of Spanish rice would be gone, the crispy coating at the bottom of the saucepan, the best part.

As noted, some days she was off. Some days she was way off. I fished a dumpling out of the pot sometime back in the '60s that has put me off of chicken stew ever since. That one day the woman could serve such a sumptuous feast and the next day make something that would leave us bug-eyed and speechless did not make sense to my brother and sister and me. Then, one day in high school, my brother picked up the pattern. At the time, Mama was

going through the change (she and my father were late parents) and her moods, then, with the flux of her hormones, tended to swing more widely than they normally did. My brother, being older and being the rebellious teen and the target of a lot of the general anxiety in our house, keyed into the program fairly quickly. When Mama was feeling good, boy was she bad in that kitchen. She burned things, she overseasoned, she sometimes forgot to cook at all and served up her famous "will-a-pears." ("You've seen them before and they will appear again.") When Mama was feeling foul, being an absolute bitch on wheels, on those nights she could be the head chef at the Ritz. I swoon remembering her braised pork chops or the lemonade she would stir up on a hot summer afternoon. The family was dealing with a tough trade-off here, because when this woman was in a bad mood, the most luscious skillet spaghetti in the world (key to preparation: cheese on top, only!) mightn't make up for the cuff on the ear that might be served as an appetizer.

Sundays and holidays belonged to my father. He'd start the day fixing an enormous breakfast, which I vaguely remember included lots and lots of pancakes and bacon and sausage and fruit and toast and coffee. Vaguely, because somewhere around the age of eight my circadian rhythms shifted and I became the quintessential night person. I wish I could share the secret with the rest of you children of the night, but I honestly have no idea how

or why I convinced my parents it just wasn't worth the trouble to get little Dave out of bed on Sunday morning. In any case, with the exception of the odd strip of crispy cold bacon, any remnant of the feast that the rest of the clan had devoured had long since been cleared before I showed my face.

A rectangular aluminum pan that covered both the front and the back burner served as the primary weapon in my father's kitchen arsenal. I believe that this monstrosity is technically referred to as a griddle, although unlike the heavy, flat, one-burner job my father used for pancakes (also known as a griddle) this one had steeper sides, and rather than a long rubberlike handle, a metal flap graced each end. A turn in the kitchen generally included my father absentmindedly grabbing those noninsulated appendages and then heaping upon said pan an entire array of expletives that I myself would prefer not to repeat.

This griddle was an aesthetic nightmare. What I thought as a child was black enamel, a thought I retained until I was old enough to be considered worthy of even being allowed to get close to such a treasure, under examination in the kitchen sink proved to be a hearty baked-on crust of creosote and tarnish and petrified grease that felt to the touch the same way a barnacled ship must. Inside, however, it remained (remains) in good shape to this day, though even then it bowed in a way that sent most of the

food cascading toward the center, more or less avoiding the inconvenience of being heated by either element.

Many Sunday afternoons my father could be found quite contentedly tossing his assembled ingredients into the pan to be . . . I believe the contemporary term is "stir-fried," though what he did to this food had about as much to do with stir-frying as a Conestoga wagon does with a Jeep Cherokee. Frankly, much of what emerged from his griddle was abysmal. One of my father's closest friends owned and was the primary chef in one of the best Chinese restaurants in St. Louis. Mr. Yim would often give my father meticulous instructions on how to prepare some dish we all particularly had enjoyed, and invariably, my father would turn out something that sort of looked like and sort of tasted like *ho toy kow* (the specialty of the house) but didn't quite meet that mark. Thankfully, my father had lots of friends in the restaurant business. I remember many afternoons spent in the high-ceilinged carryout (a "duck and noodles," as his friends in the trade called such enterprises) of his friend, George Wing. A row of ceiling fans with enormous black blades spun above us as we sat in the red leather booths waiting while George and my father visited. I know now that many of these places had not been remodeled since the 1940s, and I also know that this is the reason I feel an odd warm connection to the set decoration in film noir. If we were lucky, and we almost

always were, we would carry home with us a sack full of fried rice and egg foo young. The griddle would lie blessedly dormant another week in its hiding place in the broiler part of the stove.

But I am not about wallowing in the best-forgotten parts of my father's culinary habits. Let's get back to the good stuff: the ribs. Bottom line: Daddy was a ribs man.

Before we go any further, I must draw a line in the sand. Barbecue means ribs, and ribs means big, meaty spareribs with the tips cooked on and then removed before serving, and it means a hearty red sauce with lots of molasses and as spicy as you can stand it. "Baby backs" and brisket and beef ribs and vinegar sauce and the rest of that kind of crap: Call it what you like, but don't call it barbecue.

Back in the '60s my father's proudest acquisition was not a new car but rather an oil-barrel barbecue pit, the barrel split in half the tall way and then fitted with a hinge and a mesh grill. Another unaesthetic appliance to be sure, but one that turned out the best food on earth. Did he have a secret marinade or did he use a special kind of fuel or did he have a separate basting sauce that made his ribs so special? I couldn't begin to tell you. I just know that I am a better man today from having eaten my share of those ribs over all those summers. Like everyone in my family, the last barbecue of the year, cooked and served sometime in late September, only heightened the autumnal sadness we

all felt at the beginning of another school year and the pending onslaught of winter.

In this way my father's Chinese spareribs stood in as our winter reminder of the summers past and to come, but they also stood as their own delicious treat.

Here is what I know about their preparation:

You take those same large, meaty spareribs that you use on the grill and clean them the way you would for barbecuing. (A big hint out there to all the many bogus barbecue joints in America: Fresh from the butchering, the back of the sparerib is covered with a thin, white [almost transparent] membrane. This *must* be removed *before* cooking.) You do a bunch of other stuff to the ribs, too, in terms of marinating them to be tender, but remember, I didn't pay attention to that part. I have dim memories of quantities of vinegar being involved.

Then you get out the meat ax. Each slab is first separated from its mates (an absolute no-no when barbecuing) and then chopped lengthwise into approximately thirds. You may get halves down at the short end. (You could probably have the butcher do this, though a big part of the rigmarole of preparation day was all the chopping that had to be done: It was important to my father that you know that he *worked* to prepare a meal. If he'd had to butcher the hog himself, he'd have been in hog heaven, pun perhaps intended.) Parboil the ribs until they turn the ugly gray color of wet newspaper.

For the next step you coat the ribs with a mixture that includes, as best my sister and I can figure, white flour, lots of fresh minced garlic, fresh minced green onions, salt, pepper, soy sauce, and . . . and . . . and . . . the secret ingredient(s). MSG? More vinegar? An egg? I'm sure I could list another dozen or so plausible suspects. When properly prepared the batter should be a consistency close to wallpaper paste, though that analogy is both not quite correct and grossly unappetizing. So let's dance around it a bit more. It should be:

Wetter than floured chicken but dryer than pancake batter.

Stiffer than cake mix but tackier than cookie dough.

Thinner than oatmeal but thicker than grits.

About like Cream of Wheat, maybe, except I like my breakfast cereal with noticeable chewy lumps in it, an actual pleasing holdover of my mother's happy mornings in the kitchen.

Whatever, all of this gets fried to a golden brown and served with rice and a vegetable that you select because you don't care if it's roundly ignored.

Language, like cooking, is a medium of approximation. My pinch of salt means your teaspoon and a half. Your not-to-be-missed treat just might turn my stomach. What can I tell you? It could be that, like all romantics, I suffer from that trashiest form of nostalgia of all, the misty memory of

meals gone by. Maybe, but I don't think so. My father's Chinese spareribs were the food of the Gods. This is as close to a factual statement as any I have ever made in my life.

Daddy's moved on to that big barbecue pit in the sky, and with him he took his secret ingredients. My sister and I tweak and fiddle with our own versions of Chinese spareribs, but to no avail. I don't think we'll ever get it exactly right. And just here you might expect me to leave my admonition to the younger generations to get out those three-by-five cards and capture their families' culinary heritage before it is too late. But I won't do that. You see, I don't in fact believe that is possible. I don't know that there is one thing Daddy could have taught us that would have made our ribs the wonder that his were. What's missing from our cooking is him. He *was* the secret ingredient.

Now, before the antisentimentalists gag, I should say that I don't at all mean that his special dish tasted especially good because he was the one who made it. What I'm saying instead is that I believe that each of us who cooks has one meal that is ours alone. We own it. Others can imitate or simulate, but they can never exactly replicate. Think of all the times you've followed a recipe to the letter, only to have your ravioli filling come out anemic or your chili to have decidedly little punch. That's the way it goes. Maybe you just aren't a chili person.

Yet even as I admit that my father was the rib king, the

search continues. Somewhere out there in the universe, there exists somebody else who whips up a Chinese spare-rib every bit as delicious as Daddy's. My sister claims there is a restaurant in the northwest suburbs of Chicago that comes mighty close. I'm planning an excursion for later this spring.

In the meantime the great blessing we all have is that, according to the scientists, our most enduring memories are taste and smell. I believe this. I can still taste the snicker-doodles that we got for a snack in kindergarten and the amazing ceviche I ate at a small restaurant outside of Mexico City. I intend to use this gift to make do until the rib ship once again docks in my harbor. I close my eyes and think back and I can do it. I can. I'm salivating even now. I can taste and smell the offerings of that ancient griddle just as if a fresh batch were whipped up this afternoon.

Don't Ask, Just Eat

A friend of mine once drank down a live bee with his Coke. This was on a dare (what else?), and happily the bee, in its buzzing blooming confusion, did not think to sting my friend in the throat and asphyxiate him. Instead it bumbled fitfully about until done in by digestive juices, leaving my friend to tell the tale. He had been to the Valley of Death. He had eaten the Inedible. An astounding story.

Yet when I imagine telling it to my immigrant father, I imagine him laughing, mostly, more amused than amazed as he himself sips the brains from a fish head; next comes its eyeballs. After all, he grew up in China, where

people eat the innards of live snakes which I've seen too; but such is our generation gap: I was thinking the whole time about taking pictures, whereas for my father this would have been like getting out his camera at the local health store to take a picture of spirulena, say, or brewer's yeast. Crazy food, that's all, he would have shrugged. Food some people believe in, but that he himself wouldn't pay money for.

He is not easily grossed out, and all my life I have noodled on this fact and on questions of edibility in genera. For these are what come with a move, such as my family has made, from a culture of scarcity to a culture of abundance. My parents were from rich families in China. They were not the ones who ate tree leaves during famines. But a culture intimate with famine is a culture that, even in its upper reaches, never forgets food. It is a culture that lavishes food on guests exactly because there is not enough food. It is a culture that wastes no food at home. And it is a culture that defines food broadly but prepares it with surpassing finesse—a contrast that I love. I love what it says about what it means to be beauty-loving and human in a grindingly indifferent world. I love the aesthetic sophistication involved, and the fetishistic skill.

So when a friend's parents describe to me a completely inedible banquet of unidentifiable sea creatures they were served in Singapore, I am privately hurt that they have rejected such brave labor. I think how delicious

my father would have no doubt found this meal; I recall a kind of soft-bellied sea turtle my mother loves, which is served in soup, claws and all. Even today it transports her, madeleine like, to her girlhood. I myself have enjoyed donkey dumplings and rabbit ears and fish lips, without ill effects.

On the other hand I admit that I, too, knew a certain horror when, on a recent trip to China, I was presented with a lovely dish of silkworm larvae. A quick turn of the built-in lazy Susan—a ubiquitous feature of Chinese restaurants these days—and there they were before me, so gorgeous in a greenish bowl that offset their glistening curls, that I at first registered them as most appetizing. Those appealing pop-it-in proportions, after all. Plus they were plumply crispy in a way that promised an exquisite slight-crunch-giving-way-to-juicy-middle experience.

Then I realized they were bugs.

Don't ask, just eat, my mother used to say—the best advice she ever gave me, and not something her mother had to tell her. But this is what's happened in a generation, something she never would have expected: Her children have so much, do so much, think so much that they have to be taught how to enjoy the delicious.

Entrée Nous

I love food. Food movies, food novels, food just-about-anything. Love cookbooks. Like everything about cooking, including the shopping, the peeling, the slicing, the colors, the smells. I pop open a pod of garlic with a small cheap knife I love, and when the smell drifts up, I'm in sensory bliss.

I like to eat, too, but regarding food, really, it's the imagined pleasures to come I particularly go for. In moments of dead time at the dentist, say, waiting for the Novocain to kick in, I sit with the drool towel at my chin and, facing a poster exhorting patients to floss, imagine dishes. Dishes I've cooked and want to try again, new ones

to try, menus to serve. Staring at color photos of the ravaged gums of a nonflosser, I close my eyes and imagine slices of the rare, garlicky leg of lamb I once fixed, next to perfectly tender but not mushy pan-roasted asparagus. Or maybe pillows of ravioli covered in homemade tomato sauce; possibly a perfect spinach, grapefruit, and avocado salad; that Patricia Wells chicken-in-vinegar I fixed for friends and can't wait to do again . . . for the exact right combination of people. I figure out who and how many—eight total suits me best—then place them around my table. I light the candles, turn on the music, and Oh, my. The perfect event. A dinner party.

I live in the nation's capital. Recently an old friend who grew up in the same Mississippi Delta town I did came for a visit. And so I gave a dinner party, the guest list of which was confined to people who grew up in that town, plus partners and spouses. We had a fine time, reminiscing, laughing, applying lessons we were—sometimes silently—taught back then, to what seemed to us to have become the larger truth of what we know now. I fixed broiled pork tenderloins coated in rosemary, olive oil, and garlic, covered with an apricot-mustard sauce. It was one of those transporting evenings I glue in my mind's scrapbook to go back and visit every now and then.

The next day I woke with food, the past, and the Delta on my mind: three good things. But, I thought back, I wasn't born to this dreamy culinary fantasizing, now was

I? My parents cooked, and cooked pretty well, but for them food wasn't the point. Nobody in their social circle had dinner parties. For one thing, the night meal was called "supper." For another, their gatherings weren't so much parties as occasions for uproar, bad behavior, and the dangers of no telling what. "More!" was their motto, excess the only gauge they trusted. If they had a philosophy, it was "Use it up now before it all runs out." My parents' ideal world did not include planting vegetables or putting food by. We bought, ate, bought more.

Friday nights, Mama and Daddy cooked a steak with their friends. That was how they said it. "Let's cook a steak." Great big T-bones. Bourbon, garlic bread, some salad. The steaks were about two inches thick, dark red, lushly marbled. When it was my parents' turn to cook, my father would bring the meat home from the butcher, take the steaks out of their white waxed paper, and spread them on a metal pan to marinate in a blend of olive oil and soy sauce. My mother did the garlic bread: soft loaves of un-sliced, bullet-shaped white bread, slashed on the diagonal into thick slices, filled with melted butter and freshly chopped garlic poured from a metal pan, until the bread filled up and oozed bright yellow. She also made the salad and sometimes a vegetable. No dessert. Booze was all the sweets they needed. Besides, by the time the steaks had been dispensed with, nobody would be able to hold onto a thought, much less digest more food.

These were our peak years, financially speaking. We lived in a two-story house we built, the only house we ever owned, in the Mississippi town where we lived for the twelve years of my elementary- and high-school education. During that brief home-owning phase, my father ran a business. He had an office, a secretary. He no longer hit the road as a traveling salesman every Monday, and life was good. We lived in a house with no landlord and nobody to tell us to move whenever they felt like it. Or so I thought, not knowing about banks and mortgages and notes come due.

The plot of the Friday-night steak cook was always the same. For a child, certainty is comforting. The child lies in bed thinking, *Oh good, I know about this.* Dread can be a tonic, no matter the dangers ahead. By the time Daddy got home with the steaks, he might have already dropped by the Yacht Club for a drink and some stories, so he'd be a little juiced up. He'd sing, dance, do a little jig. Man, oh man, at that very moment he was happy. He'd have made a trip out to the county line, to the bootlegger's. From upstairs in my flowered-wallpapered room, I could hear the muffled clank as the paper-sacked bottle hit the kitchen counter. Then a clink of glasses, and my father's throaty "Aaaaghhh"—which sounded half like pleasure and half like a groan of deep pain—as he threw down his first shot. That was the signal, as concretely preordained as a fire-drill bell: Friday night had begun.

My mother drank toddies, sugared-up bourbon with warm water and a slice of orange. When she came down, he'd fix her one or two. She'd admire the steaks, maybe ask him why he was late. They might have a row; he might end it by saying "Awwww...Mama!" like a boy whose mother has told him he can't go to the picture show. She might storm upstairs and slam the door.

My mother was pretty and blond and small and blue-eyed. She could make her thick straight hair roll into a perfect pageboy, which I, with my wispy-lank locks, envied. After the slamming of the door, she would shower and dress and fix her face, sitting in front of the mahogany dresser with the oval mirror, facing her tantalizing potions: the boxes of Coty face powder, the tubes of Cherries in the Snow lipstick, the red Maybelline eyebrow pencils, the curvy bottles of Emeraude perfume. I loved watching her mouth when she put the lipstick on, how elastic it got when she swiped the tube over the bottom lip.

This was in the mid '50s, and back then nobody drank wine with dinner. Beer was a thirst quencher that men used as a chaser or guzzled fast on a hot day after a golf game. To my parents and their friends, drinking meant bourbon—and a lot of it. Those days nobody called himself an alcoholic, nobody thought about quitting drinking, no matter the smashed cars, lost legs, lost jobs, unhappy children. People just drank. Had fights, broke windows, slept, got up. Drank more.

They cooked steak on a Friday so they could stay drunk all weekend. The T-bone was like holy water, christening the blessed blotto part of their week. People arrived half-stewed. There were usually two other couples, maybe three. They drank more. At about nine or ten, my father would start the fire and cook the steaks.

The sequence of events those Friday nights never changed. People drank until they were drunk, ate, drank more, and then something terrible happened. When I wrote a novel about a Mississippi Delta dinner party, I didn't have to worry about plot. I relied on what I knew. The plot had been outlined for me long years before. Drink, eat, drink, *bam!*

When Daddy was finished cooking, he brought the T-bones in with great fanfare and everybody sat down to eat. They ate, drank. Drank, ate. When the meal was over they usually went in the living room to the piano where my mother played "Darktown Strutters Ball" and "Glowworm," or my father sang "Say It Isn't So." And somewhere along in there, the terrible thing happened. It might be momentous or nothing, serious or slight. It was always loud. Somebody might storm out and slam the door, vowing never to speak to any of them again. Somebody might hitch up his pants and throw a punch. A woman might hurl an ashtray at her husband and hit the window instead. *Bam!*

I lay in my bed with my movie magazine or a new

Nancy Drew, staring at the diamond-shaped patterns of flowers on my wall. I hoped the noise and trouble would ease on down and be over soon, but more important, that it wouldn't be my parents' voices I heard rising to that terrible pitch and tempo, which I think of now as "the bulldog roll." They sounded so wild, like trained pets who suddenly revealed their true natures. The wailing of a bitch cat in heat, the snarl of a sweet-tempered dog suddenly cornered and threatened. Once the roll started it didn't stop until the terrible thing occurred. And that was the end of it. Car engines roared, tires screeched. I looked out my window hoping to find our car still in the driveway. Sometimes it was.

When I grew up and left home, I based my perception of what a dinner party was on what I knew. In my early twenties I lived in New York City. I was married with a baby. When we went to dinner parties or gave them, and people sat around the table having a conversation, I did what I could to liven things up. Balance the butter plate on my head, get out the broom and stage a limbo contest. I wasn't violent like my parents. I never flung raw steaks around the way my mother was said to have done at the Yacht Club following some intimacy either real or imagined between my father and I have no idea which other woman. I performed small tricks or talked racy, turned up the music, and said, "Oh, let's dance." I wanted something to happen. Conversation didn't count. Talk was boring.

My parents never cleaned up on Friday night. They left everything for the next morning. When I came down plates were still on the table, steaks half-eaten, slabs of tooth-marked bread afloat in congealed butter. The smell of the garlic was strong but not as powerful as the fumes of bourbon that filled up the house like fire. I walked right past the table. Ate my toast facing the backyard.

Saturdays, everybody backtracked. There were phone calls, apologies, remorse, and recriminations. The new shirt bloodied and cut to ribbons was replaced. The black eye nursed, the hangover, the swollen ankle from a fall . . . Daddy played golf. Mama cleaned up. The dog gnawed in T-bone heaven. Somebody made another trip to the bootlegger's. That night they usually went out, maybe to the Yacht Club to play poker or to Doe's Eat Place for tamales. Sunday we went to church as a family and my parents began winding the weekend down. That night we'd cook another steak, this time for family only. And my brother and I would sit with my mother and father as if Friday night hadn't happened. As if we were all happy, and life was easy, and this was normal, and we would always live in the two-story house, and I would always have my flowered wallpaper, and Daddy would not have to go on the road or work on commission ever again.

A woman I met in New York taught me to cook and to love food in a more patient and extravagant way. It took a lot of years but gradually I began moving away from the

role I thought I'd been born to play—that of party clown—toward the possibility of seeing myself as a thoughtful person. A radical idea for a southern girl, unless she's also willing to think of herself as an unattractive dog of a woman. Didn't happen fast. Shucking your parents' lessons never does.

Anyway I didn't want to change. Not that I liked uproar and trouble; on the contrary. But chaos was familiar; the smell of bourbon, my madeleine. I depended on the *bam!* to remind me where I came from and, therefore, I assumed, who I was. But in time I became adventurous enough to flirt with uncertainty and to risk the unknown. My dinner parties settled down. I took the butter plate off my head.

The pre-meal conversation at my recent Delta reunion party was so exciting and edgy, so satisfying and funny and even, from time to time, dangerous. I couldn't stand to miss out on a word. It wasn't my best meal. I lost track of time and overcooked the pork and the asparagus. Never mind. I lit the candles. We sat at the table and talked and talked, our shared pasts illuminating the present like distant snuffling candles. Beyond the windows, way out there on the other side of the trees, their flickering glow beckoned but threw so little and such angry light that we had no desire to follow. Only to remember.

The Burden
of the Feast

This Christmas my two sisters and my brother and I, along with our families, will head toward home, our real home, which is where our seventy-eight-year-old mother, Christy, lives, in western Kentucky. She'll be ready for us with the usual Christmas feast, and what I'm looking forward to most is the green beans and sweet potatoes and creamed corn, the farm fare that once seemed so oppressively ordinary to me. When I was growing up on our fifty-three-acre dairy farm, we were obsessed with food. Food was the center of our lives. Everything we did, every day, revolved around it. We planted it, grew it, harvested it, peeled it, cooked it, served it, consumed it—endlessly, day after day,

season after season. This was life on a farm. I can appreci-
ate the value of a country upbringing now, but when I was
a girl all that toil drove me crazy.

One day my mother and my grandmother were
shelling beans and talking about the proper method of
drying apples. I was eleven and entirely absorbed with the
March girls in *Little Women*. Drying apples was not in my
dreams. Beth's death was weighing darkly on me at that
moment, and I threw a little tantrum—what Mama called
a hissy fit.

"Can't y'all talk about anything but food?" I screamed.

There was a shocked silence. "Well, what else is
there?" Granny asked.

Granny didn't question her duties, but I did. I didn't
want to be hulling beans in a hot kitchen when I was fifty
years old. I wanted to be somebody, maybe an airline stew-
ardess. Also, I had been listening to the radio. I had notions.

Life for our family was haunted by the fear of crop
failure. We ate as if we didn't know where our next meal
might come from. All my life I have had a recurrent food
dream: I face a buffet or cafeteria line, laden with beauti-
ful foods. I spend the entire dream choosing the foods I
want. The anticipation of eating them is deliciously ago-
nizing. I always wake up just as I've made my selections
but before I get to eat.

Working with food was fraught with anxiety and des-
peration when I was a girl. Like all farmers we were at the

mercy of the weather, and it wasn't to be trusted. My mother watched the skies at evening for any portent of the morrow. A cloud that went over and then turned around and came back was an especially bad sign. Our livelihood—even our lives—depended on forces outside our control.

I think this dependence on nature was at the core of my rebellion. I hated the constant sense of helplessness before vast forces, the continuous threat of failure. Farmers didn't take the initiative, I began to see; they reacted to whatever presented itself. More than that, though, I disliked women's part in that dependence.

My mother had been raised in a large farm family— kinfolks who had taken her in when she was orphaned— but they had little time for her. One Christmas the only present she got was an orange, while her cousins got dolls. Her life had been hard, and so she allowed me to get spoiled. She never even tried to teach me to cook. "You didn't want to learn," she says now. "You were always busy doing something. You had your nose in a book."

From the front yard, where I sat reading under a maple tree, I could see my mother stooped over in the garden and my father on his tractor, far back in the field. No wonder I believed that progress meant freedom from the field and the range. That meant moving to town, I thought. Because we lived only a mile outside the town of Mayfield, I was acutely conscious of being country. I felt

inferior to people in town because we had to grow our food and make our clothes; we couldn't just go buy things, the way they did. Although we were self-sufficient and resourceful and held clear title to our land, we farm people lived in a state of psychological poverty. We felt that the fine life in town—celebrated in magazines, on radio, in movies—was denied us. Of course, we weren't poor at all—I knew that. Poor people had too many kids, and they weren't landowners; they rented decrepit little houses with plank floors and trash in the yard. "Poor people are wormy and eat wild onions," Mama said. We weren't poor, but we were country.

We had three wardrobes—everyday clothes, school clothes, and Sunday clothes. We didn't wear our school clothes at home, but we could wear them to town. When we got home from church, we had to change back into everyday before we ate Mama's big Sunday dinner. "Don't eat in your good clothes!" Mama always cried. "You'll spill something on them."

The truth was, Mama was a natural cook. At harvest time, after she'd got in from the garden and put out a wash, she would whip up a noontime dinner for the men in the field—my father and grandfather and maybe some neighbors and a couple of hired hands: fried chicken with milk gravy, ham, mashed potatoes, lima beans, field peas, corn, slaw, sliced tomatoes, fried apples, biscuits, and

peach pie. This was not considered a banquet, only plain hearty food, fuel for work. All the ingredients except the flour, sugar, and salt came from the farm—the chickens, the hogs, the milk and butter, the potatoes from the potato patch, the beans, peas, corn, cabbage, apples, peaches. Nothing was processed, except by her. She was always butchering and plucking and planting and hoeing and shredding and slicing and creaming (scraping cobs for the creamed corn), and pressure-cooking and canning and freezing and thawing and mixing and shaping and baking and frying.

We were known to eat our pie right on the same plate as our turnip greens so as not to mess up another dish. It didn't matter if the peach cobbler oozed all over the turnip-green juice and the pork grease. "It all goes to the same place," Mama said. We never used napkins, and our table manners were boarding-house reach—no "Pass the peas, please." Conversation detracted from the sensuous pleasure of filling yourself. Every meal required meat and vegetables and dessert. We drank milk and iced tea ("ice-tea"). Our salads were fruit Jell-O and slaw. We also ate "poke salet" and wilted lettuce. Mama picked tender young pokeweed in the woods in the spring, before it turned poison, and cooked it a long time to get the bitterness out. We liked it with vinegar and minced boiled eggs. Wilted lettuce was tender new lettuce, shredded, with sliced radishes

and green onions, and blasted with hot bacon grease to blanch the rawness. "Too many fresh vegetables in the summer gives people the scours," Daddy said.

July was blackberry-picking time. Mama would come back from the fields, where patches of "tame" berries had spread along the fencerows and creek banks, and exclaim, "There are worlds of berries down there!" She always "engaged" the berries to customers. By June, she would say, "I've already got forty gallons of berries engaged."

We strode out at dawn, in the dew, and picked until the midmorning sun bore down on our heads. To protect her hands from the thorns. Mama made gloves from old bluejeans, with the fingertips cut out. Following the berries down onto the creek bank, we perched on ledges and tiptoed on unsure footing through thickets. We tunneled. When Mama saw an especially large berry just out of reach, she would lean her body against the bush and let it support her while she plucked the prize. We picked in quart baskets, then poured the berries into red-and-white Krey lard buckets. The berries settled quickly and Mama picked an extra quart to top off the buckets. By nine o'clock the sun was high, and I struggled to the house with my four gallons of blackberries, eager to wash the chiggers off and eat some cereal.

From the blackberries, I learned about money. I wouldn't eat the berries, even on my cereal: I wanted the

money from selling them. Granny said everything was food, but I was hungry for something else—a kind of food that didn't grow in the ground. Yet I couldn't deny that we were always feasting. We ate sumptuous meals, never missing dessert. At Christmas we slurped gallons of boiled custard. Once in a while, Daddy brought home exotic treats—fried oysters in little goldfish cartons and hot tamales wrapped in corn shucks.

Food was better in town, we thought. It wasn't plain and ordinary and everyday. The main pleasures were there, too—the barbecue places, the movie shows, all the places to buy things. Woolworth's, with the pneumatic tubes overhead rushing money along a metallic mole tunnel up to a balcony. Lochridge & Ridgway, with an engraved sign on the third-story cornice: STOVES, APPLIANCES, PLOWS. On the mezzanine at that store, I bought my first phonograph records, brittle 78s of big-band music—Woody Herman and Glenn Miller, and Glen Gray and his Casa Loma Orchestra playing "No Name Jive." A circuit of the square took you past the grand furniture stores, the two dime stores, the ladies' stores, the banks, the drugstores. You'd walk past the poolroom and an exhaust fan would blow the intoxicating smell of hamburgers in your face. Before she bought a freezer, Mama kept our meat in a rented food locker in town, near the ice company. She stored the butchered calf there and she fetched hunks each week to fry. But hamburgers in town were

better. They were greasier and they came in waxed-paper packages.

At the corner drugstore, on the courthouse square, Mama and my younger sister Janice and I sat at filigreed wrought-iron tables on a black-and-white mosaic tile floor, eating peppermint ice cream. It was cold in there, under the ceiling fans. The ice cream was served elegantly, in paper cones sunk into black plastic holders. We were uptown.

In the summer of 1954, when I was about to enter high school, my mother got a chance to run a restaurant not far from our house, up on Highway 45. My parents knew the owner, and one day he stopped by and asked Mama if she'd like to manage it. She jumped at the opportunity to earn some money. "Why, anybody could cook hamburgers and french fries for the public," Mama said confidently. "That would be easy."

She was eager for a chance to buy us things. After the war, she had wanted Daddy to get out of dairy farming and run a small business of some kind, something that would bring in more cash, but he had refused to leave his parents' farm. He was an only child and my grandparents depended on him to carry on. Mama had swallowed her disappointment. She was resilient and optimistic—when Janice and I were growing up, we always saw her sparkling like morning dew—and she always wanted more for her children.

She went to inspect the Mayfield Restaurant—a square cinder-block building with a picture-window view of the highway. There were no trees around, just a graveled parking area. It was an informal sort of place, with a simple kitchen in back, a few pots and pans, a deep fryer, and a grill. There were five or six tables and a counter with stools. Mama saw potential. "Catfish platters," she said, with her face alight. "Fish and hush puppies. Slaw. French fries."

I was so excited I couldn't sleep. Running our own little restaurant could mean we wouldn't have to work in the garden. I wanted nothing more to do with okra and beans. I longed for deliverance and an endless supply of Co'–Colas.

A restaurant would hold no fears for her. "It's a chance to make big money," she told me. She told the owner she would try it for two weeks. If she liked the work, the deal was, she would be permitted to rent the business, for a hundred dollars a month.

"If it works out, maybe I could make a hundred dollars a *week*," she said.

I tagged along. I felt important waiting on customers—strangers driving along the highway and stopping right where I was for a bite to eat. I wanted to meet somebody from New York. When I drew glasses of Coca-Cola from the fountain, the Coke fizzed over crushed ice. I made grilled-cheese sandwiches in the grilled-cheese machine. I experimented with milk shakes. I was flying.

Most of all, I loved the jukebox. The first week Mama was there, the jukebox man came by to change records and insert new red-rimmed paper strips of titles: Doris Day and Johnnie Ray duets; "Teardrops from My Eyes," by Ruth Brown; and "P.S. I Love You," by a Kentucky vocal group called the Hilltoppers. I listened avidly to everything. I was fourteen and deeply concerned about my suntan, and I was saving pocket money to buy records.

The restaurant also had a television set, which sat in a corner with a "television light" on top—a prism of soft colors that supposedly kept people from ruining their eyes on TV waves. I had no experience with television and I was captivated by Donald O'Connor's variety show and *I Love Lucy*. When the evening crowd came in, Mama was kept busy as she trotted back and forth from the kitchen with her hamburger platters and catfish platters, but she would stop and laugh at something Lucy and Ethel were doing on the screen.

Two days before the trial period was up, Mama stopped going to the restaurant. She didn't give up the job voluntarily. My grandfather had stepped in and told her she couldn't go on. "We need you here at home," he said. "Running a hamburger joint out on the highway ain't fitten' work."

Daddy—who had his own part-time job, delivering milk for a dairy—didn't stand up for her. "How would you

make any money, anyway?" he demanded. "By the time you pay out that hundred dollars a month rent and all the expenses, you won't have nothing left. First thing you know, you'll get behind and then you'll be owing *him*."

Granny said, "And who's going to do your cooking here at home?"

Mama didn't mention the restaurant again, but I thought I saw a little fire go out of her. My own flame was burning brighter. I had had a glimpse of life outside the farm, and I wanted it. I can still see Mama emerging from that restaurant kitchen, carrying two hamburger platters and gabbing with her customers as if they were old friends who had dropped in to visit and sit a spell. In the glass of the picture window, reflections from the television set flicker like Christmas candles.

JILL McCORKLE

Her Chee-to Heart

If I could have a perfect day of eating, this would be it: I'd begin with pancakes and sausage patties drenched in Log Cabin syrup. Then I'd visit my grandmother's kitchen, where my sister and I used to watch ravenously as Gramma made her famous pound cake (a real pound cake—a pound of butter, a pound of sugar, egg after egg after egg swirled in Swans Down cake flour). We'd each slurp batter off the mixer whisks and then split what was left in the red-and-white Pyrex bowl. My grandmother also made chicken and pastry (her pastry was more like dumplings) and homemade biscuits (the secret ingredient is lard), which might be dipped in redeye gravy or covered

in butter and Karo syrup (doughboys) and eaten as dessert. She made homemade apple pies (the fruit part of our diet) fried in Crisco and filled with sugar.

If I couldn't have homemade food, then I would settle for what could be bought. A foot-long hot dog at the B&R Drive-In, for example; french fries limp with grease and salt from the bowling alley; a barbecue sandwich (Carolina style—chopped fine and spiced up with hot sauce); a triple-chocolate milk shake from Tastee-Freez. Banana splits and hot-fudge sundaes. Maybe a frozen Zero candy bar or a Milky Way, a Little Debbie snack cake and a moon pie, too.

I am a junk-food junkie and always have been. My college roommate and my husband both blame me for their slides into high-fat, preservative-filled meals, like the frozen Mexican TV dinners that my roommate and I ate all the way through college, or the microwavable burritos I now stash at the back of my freezer for desperate moments (desperate meaning a craving for Tex-Mex or a need to drive a nail and not being able to find a hammer). Forget meals, anyway; the truly good treats for a junk-food junkie get served up in between: colorful Ben & Jerry's pints, natural in an ethical way (the money goes to good places, at least) that makes me feel healthy; names— Chubby Hubby, Chunky Monkey, Wavy Gravy—that make me laugh. Good Humor is what it's all about and has been since childhood: kids trained to respond to the

ringing of a bell, to chase alongside trucks in neighbor-
hood streets like so many pups for a Nutty Buddy. Ice
cream is near the top of any junk-food junkie's list to be
sure, but I haven't even begun to mention the Chee-tos,
the Pecan Sandies.

There's something about unnatural food colors that
has always attracted me. What tastes or looks better than
the frosting on grocery-store–bakery birthday cakes? Hot
pink or blue roses that melt in your mouth. The fluores-
cent brilliance of a crunchy Chee-to. Not too long ago my
children (ages four and seven) were eating at a friend's.
They were served a lovely meal of homemade macaroni
and cheese, white, the way something without any addi-
tives and preservatives should be. I was on the other side
of the room, helpless to defend myself when I heard my
daughter say, "But my mom's macaroni and cheese is
bright orange." Well? What can I say? I also love that
fuchsia-colored sweet-and-sour sauce that you often find
on Chinese food buffets.

At the last big dinner party we had, my husband
bought Yodels to throw out on the dessert table along
with a fresh-fruit concoction, which had taken me forever
to cut up, and little cheesecakes. At the end of the night,
there was not a Yodel in sight, but very few people had
openly indulged. These scrumptious lunch-box treats
(creme-filled chocolate rolls, 140 calories and 8 grams of
fat each, which means, of course, that they are good) had

instead been slyly tucked away into pockets and purses for the ride home. Yodels, Twinkies, Hostess Snoballs. They make people nostalgic for elementary school, those wonderful years when we were advised to eat beef and pork. Children thriving on sloppy joes and Saturday T-bones. Pork chops with applesauce. Sausage gravy over homemade biscuits. A good green vegetable in the South, where I grew up, was a green-bean casserole in which the beans were camouflaged in Campbell's cream of mushroom soup and canned fried onion rings. All the recipes in my favorite cookbooks begin with Campbell's cream-of-something soup.

I was enamored of a boy named Michael in the first grade who licked Kool-Aid powder from his palm whenever the teacher wasn't looking. He moved away before the end of the year, and yet thirty-one years later, I still remember him with a fond mixture of repulsion at the sticky red saliva that graced his notebook paper and admiration for the open ease with which he indulged his habit. I loved Pixy Stix straws, which, let's face it, were nothing more than dry Kool-Aid mix poured right into your mouth. Sweetarts. Jawbreakers. Firecrackers. Mary Janes. Any item that I was told was *very* bad for my teeth.

Maybe it's an oral-gratification thing. I'm sure that's why I smoked for fifteen years. When I quit nine years ago, I rediscovered my taste buds. I found flavors I had forgotten all about: Sugar Babies and Raisinets, that thick

mashed-potato gravy that is the *real* secret ingredient at
Kentucky Fried Chicken. I found flavors I had never had
before, such as cheese blintzes and latkes smothered in
sour cream. I found that wonderful, all-natural, fortified
cereal Quaker 100% Natural Oats Honey and Raisins. I
need oral participation, oral gratification. Despite what
they will tell you on television, a little stick of Juicy Fruit
is not going to get you there if you've been lighting up for
years. But M&M's? Junior Mints? Those diablo-style
peanuts thoroughly doused with cayenne pepper? Now,
that's chewing satisfaction. A Coke (or diet Coke for the
figure-minded; Jolt cola for the desperate-to-start-the-
day-minded) chaser.

I could do a taste test. I can recognize all the sodas.
The soda wanna-bes. I drink a good two to three cups of
coffee when I get up, and by the time I drive the kids to
school, I've switched over to diet Coke. People say,
"Doesn't it keep you awake?" I wish! During one of my
pregnancies I lost all taste for Coke. I couldn't believe it.
I'd been drinking Coke for as long as I could remember. It
was so sad; filling myself up on Hawaiian Punch (which is
very good in its own right), Pop-Tarts, and ice cream, ice
cream, ice cream. But I missed the Coke cans rolling
around under the seat of my car. I missed the whoosh and
zap of buying a Coke from a vending machine. And one
day, like magic, it returned, this desire, like an old love
resurfacing.

There are ways a junk-food junkie can feel less guilty about all this food, if indeed you ever do feel guilty. Did I mention caffeine? It's like air—essential for full enjoyment. And it burns calories. If that doesn't work, there are always things like the NordicTrack where I hang my clothes at the end of the day and the Suzanne Somers Thighmaster I keep in my closet for decoration.

Besides, I consider myself a purist; I don't like substitute things—like these new clear sodas. Who cares? I went into the all-natural health-food grocery store not long ago only to discover that there are a lot of things in this world that are foreign to me. The produce section had products you might find growing in a neglected basement. There were name brands I'd never heard of; certainly they don't buy airtime on television. There were cereals without colored marshmallows or prizes in the box. They boasted of having no sugar (as if this were good). It did not take me long to get back to the familiar aisles of the Super Stop & Shop, the red-and-white Campbell's soup labels, the chip-and-cookie aisle (nothing there sweetened with fruit juice or carob imitating chocolate), and the candy bars at the checkout.

One of my fondest junk-food memories is of a rare snow day in Lumberton, North Carolina, when I was in the sixth grade, a wonderful age at which, though I liked boys, they were not nearly as exciting as the ice cream store nearby that served up an oversize cone called a

Kitchen Sink. But that day, I sat with a couple of friends in the back of the Kwik-Pik (the South's version of the convenience store) and ate raw chocolate-chip-cookie dough while drinking Eagle Brand sweetened condensed milk straight from the can. My friends and I waddled home feeling sick but warmly nourished, our stomachs coated and glowing with sugar. I mean, really, there is no cake or cookie on earth that tastes as good as dough or batter.

My favorite food in the eighth grade was Slim Jim sausages. For the uninformed, these are the miniature pepperoni sticks usually found near the register of convenience stores, where you might also find the beef jerky and pickled eggs. When I was growing up, there was usually a big jar of pickled pig's feet too, but this was not a treat that ever caught my eye. No, I lived on Slim Jims, spicy and chewy. I kept them with me at all times, getting a good chew while at cheerleading practices. They reminded me of being an even younger kid and getting a little bit of raw, salty country ham from my grandmother and chewing it all day like a piece of gum. (Sorry, Juicy Fruit; failed again.)

My husband, a doctor whose specialty is infectious diseases, is certain that I have been host to many parasites. Maybe, but what I'm certain that I have been host to are the junk-food parasites who refuse to admit that they indulge, but they do. Just put out a bowl of pistachios and check out the red fingertips leaving; chips, M&M's. Ah,

M&M's. It was a sad day long ago when they retired the red ones. I had spent years being entertained by a pack; segregate and then integrate, close your eyes and guess which color. I was thrilled when the red ones returned, and now blue! Lovely blue M&M's. I love the pastel ones at Easter, along with those Cadbury eggs, and my own personal favorite: malted Easter eggs. These are actually Whoppers (malted-milk balls) covered in a speckled candy shell. Sometimes they are called robin eggs and sometimes simply malteds, but a Whopper is a Whopper is a Whopper. I like to bite one in half and then suck in. When the air is pulled out of a Whopper, what's left is more like a Milk Dud.

Of course there is also the Whopper from Burger King. Once, after a Friday night high-school football game, I sat down at a table with a bag of food that looked similar to those of all the guys on the team. I had a Whopper with everything, large fries, an apple pie, and a chocolate shake. Our cheerleading adviser told me that I wouldn't always be able to do that.

Thank God I didn't know she was right. It would have ruined the next four years as I continued to down cream-filled Krispy Kreme doughnuts and my own special high-protein omelette that was filled with mayonnaise and cheese. I loved Funyuns, too, except that nobody wanted to sit next to me on the bus when I ate them.

After all these years, I've made some adjustments. I

now buy Hebrew National for things like hot dogs and
bologna. I figure the kosher laws probably serve me well
in this particular purchase, and try as I might to dissuade
them, my children love bologna with an absolute passion.
They can smell the reject turkey substitute from fifty
paces. They don't like *real* mac and cheese. They like the
microwave kind. My niece (at age four) once invited me
into her playhouse for lunch. She said, "Would you like a
diet Coke while I cook lunch in the microwave?" So maybe
it's a family thing. Maybe it's the potassium benzoate.

I would love a diet Coke and a cream horn right about
now. Some salt-and-vinegar chips. Onion dip and Ruffles.
S'mores. I like to get in bed to read with a stash of some-
thing close by. I have found that I am especially drawn to
things with a high polyglycerol-ester-of-fatty-acids con-
tent. It makes me feel *happy*. I think maybe this is the key
to a true junk-food junkie's heart: happiness. Just as
Proust bit into his little madeleine and had a flood of mem-
ories, I bite into my Devil Dog, my Ring-Ding, Twinkie,
Ho-Ho, Yodel. I bite into my Hostess Snoball and retreat
to a world where the only worry is what to ask your
mother to put in your lunch box the next day or which
pieces of candy you will select at the Kwik-Pik on your
way home from school. Ahead of you are the wasteland
years: a pack of cigarettes, some Clearasil pads, a tube of
Blistex, and breath spray. But for now, reach back to those
purer, those sugar-filled, melt-in-your-mouth, forever-a-

kid years. Who cares if there is a little polysorbate 60 and some diglycerides, some carrageenan, some Red 40 and Blue 1, some agar-agar? I have a dream that somewhere out there in the grown-up, low-fat world there is a boy named Michael licking his lips and getting all the fumaric acid that he can.

The Famine of Bengal

In 1942, after the Japanese armies had overrun Burma and Singapore and bombed several Indian ports, it was feared World War II would engulf India. Preparations were made for a defense of India by Allied armies rerouted from other theaters of war. To feed the expected armies, entire harvests were bought from Indian villagers who eagerly sold all their grain, even family supplies, in this once-in-a-lifetime opportunity to free themselves of debt.

When the Japanese attack did not materialize the food was released as rapidly as it had been acquired—into the hands of middlemen who controlled the black market. Throughout that winter of 1942 and into the spring of

1943, tons of food rotted away, hoarded by black marke-
teers. And three million people starved to death, most of
them on the streets of Calcutta.

As hungry peasants flooded into Calcutta in search of
work for food, restaurants did brisk business. One road-
side stall offered three options to its customers:

A price to see the food.

A higher price to smell the food.

A third price to eat the food.

After all, there was no shortage of food in the Famine
of Bengal.

It must be hard to be hungry when food is plentiful.
Hard to look at billboards advertising food, to smell cook-
ing through the doorways of restaurants, to watch people
eating on the street. Hard to see food and smell food and
not be able to eat. It must be hard to be hungry, even in
the U.S.A.

Eat Your Pets

Standing in a million acres of remote, rock-throttled, lizard-gnawed Utah desert, I think back to a recent time in southern California, when I was stuck on a freeway with three lanes of halted cars spewing several millennia of fossilized plant beds from their exhausts, the fumes popping my few remaining brain cells like bubble wrap, nearly knocking me unconscious so that if the traffic ever did move again, I, slumped over the steering wheel, dripping stalactites of drool onto the rental car's tasteful silver shag carpet, would incite gridlock anew, and the other drivers, their bloodstreams raging with espresso, would hate me and start shooting. I now stand in intense heat on alkaline

soil sprouting shrubs so sparse, thorny, scruffy, and stumpy, they seem more like green bones than plants, and remember the car ahead of me in that California traffic jam, a sleekly ovoid, Teutonic marvel with in-dash fax and Jacuzzi. Its bumper sticker said, "I'd rather be hunting and gathering."

Californians dine by a sacred creed: Eat fresh ingredients, procured locally, grown seasonally. "We don't shop at supermarkets anymore," they sniff. "We forage," and it's off to pluck zinfandel grapes and *fraises de bois* with gloves made from the underbellies of bilingual alpacas, to buy fetal aubergines from Buddhists, oysters shucked by the Holy Ghost, and olives cured in the spittle of Himalayan puppies. Even if the nation's food distribution system were suddenly paralyzed, forcing everyone to eat locally, Californians would still be pâté-plump and hot-tub poached while the rest of us stumbled about in weasel pelts. Californians may have overcrowded their own nest, but they will always eat better.

Every region in the world that has produced a flavorful, healthy cuisine, the foodies claim, has based that cuisine on local materials. Notice, however, that people are not rioting for an indigenous Northern Rockies cuisine, for example, for bloody bison blubber, jerked beaver, or tennis-ball tomatoes sponsored by hormones in a thirty-two-day frost-free season. Nor do they crave what might be procured in this parched sandstone canyon in Utah,

where I am trying to live by the Creed and prepare a meal with native resources. Compromises have been made.

We float through this canyon on a white-water raft, packing in all food and supplies, as we do in a series of trips during my husband's seasonal job as a backcountry river ranger. The wilderness must be left intact. It would be rather unseemly, not to mention illegal, for a federal agent to be tilling crops or killing possibly endangered mammals for dinner. Another reason for packing in our food is that shopping in a rural supermarket, where I supply each river trip, poses many challenges.

In a land of high birth rates, baby products consume considerable shelf space. There is a marked absence of crustaceans and a notable preponderance of "white food," such as processed sandwich spreads, prewhipped topping substances, and frisbees of pallid cheese and dough in the frozen pizza bin. There are hard balls of colorless lettuce with the charisma of a barnacle and many items in nugget form. Say "tofu" around here and everyone will think you have sinus problems. Fresh summer produce can be luscious but limited in repertoire. Good wines? One's brain hemorrhages with any attempt to explain Utah's liquor regulations, which in complexity lie one rung on the purgatorial ladder below tax laws. Nearly every election year, a citizens group launches an effort to "legalize adulthood in Utah" and ease the moral vise of an abstemious theocracy. Every year they fail.

News of a fallen Berlin Wall has not arrived here yet. We shop in a town where, in the seventh year of the worst drought in a century, with the local reservoir shrunk to the size of a hand mirror, the city council proposed to ban xeriscaping. To these devotees of suburban botanical orthodoxy, native plants constituted ecoterrorism and weeds grew only in communist plots. When we lose green lawns, they warned, democracy will crumble. In the supermarket checkout line, where one's patriotism is routinely tested, the few interesting items I scrounge have bought me exile to Bulgaria.

"Did you, like, find these *here?*" the clerk asks, holding up in "icky" position a pack of dried corn husks (for *tamales negros*) as if they were the carapaces of hundreds of sun-fried African grasshoppers. As she empties my cart we begin a food identification rite.

"Astroturf?" she asks.

"No, cilantro," I answer.

"Caulk?"

"Feta cheese."

Reversed, the rite becomes even more idiotic.

"Styrofoam?" I ask a clerk who is stocking an aisle.

"No, Wonder bread." He presses a code into his waistband beeper, the code that summons the agent who works for the Bulgarian airline.

"Sheetrock?" I ask. "Small internal combustion engine?"

"No, Velveeta. Family pack."

Despite a reputation for being meatloafed on the steppes of culinary mediocrity, the intermountain West has slowly begun to buck the cholesterol tide. My own demands are not unreasonable. I merely want reasonably fresh, flavorful, minimally carcinogenic food. I want to eat like a Fremont.

The Fremont Indians lived in the Great Basin and Colorado Plateau from around the seventh to the thirteenth century, roughly contemporary with the Southwest's fabled Anasazi. Archaeologists working on Utah's Fremont River first recognized the Fremont as a distinct variation of the Anasazi culture and gave it the name. These seminomads hunted mule deer along the river corridor where I now travel and stalked bighorn sheep in its highlands and tributary canyons. When conditions were favorable they grew squash, beans, and corn, which they stored in masonry cists under protected ledges in the canyon walls. They pecked magnificent and enigmatic rock art on the faces of sandstone boulders and cliffs, made baskets and ceramic pots, and gathered wild plants for culinary, medicinal, and ceremonial purposes. Beyond these generalizations it is reckless to define the Fremont for, like the Anasazi, they were opportunistic, diverse, and adaptable in a harsh, arid environment of great variety: mountains, alkali basins, deep canyons, juniper-pinyon forests,

and this broad, silty river wedged between thousand-foot-high cliffs.

What if, like the Fremont and Anasazi, you were entirely responsible for procuring your food from your immediate environs? What if you failed and went hungry? I cannot speak from experience because I grew up and remain well fed. We were not a "think of starving children in China" kind of family, each meal dredged in béchamel and guilt. The Great Depression was my parents' tribal history. They understood necessity and never used hunger as punishment. They never sent us to our rooms without dinner, only without dessert. If they served up a lesson with the green beans, it was to appreciate my mother's labors. While her peers tripped over their aprons in the post–World War II rush to industrial foods, my mother drew on an eclectic cuisine known in our household as "from scratch." My young lips never touched Jell-O or orange squares of petronuclear cheese smelted between two slabs of snow-white, inflatable bread.

Only as a young adult did I first see true hunger. At a city diner I once sat across the room from a shabby vagrant who was nursing a cup of coffee, the only food he could afford. When he thought no one was looking, he uncapped a bottle of ketchup set among the table condiments and drank it down like a cold beer. A vegetarian, obviously.

In the river canyon, California reverie ended, I look
around at the hunter-gatherer's larder. Cattle grazed these
river bottoms for a century, selecting for certain forage, so
there is a mix of native and exotic flora, a postgrazing
plant succession also influenced by erosion and drought.
Things are not exactly as they were a thousand years ago.
Nevertheless, the Fremont Indians would have eaten rice-
grass, squawbush berries, the greens of fourwing saltbush
or its ashes in a cornmeal-based bread. They may have
chewed the roots of globemallow to strengthen broken
bones, washed their hair with yucca root, and painted with
beeplant, cliffrose, or greasewood dyes. They used yucca
fibers for twine, cattails for mats, rabbit hair for coats.
The Fremont wore the desert; they ate it.

What would it be like to eat everything you could lay
your hands on? What if, standing on this sunny alluvial
fan spilling into the sinuous river, I were very, very hun-
gry? For a start I could stuff a few darkling beetles into my
mouth, nail the black-tailed jackrabbit under the grease-
wood bush, gnaw sugary mariposa bulbs, clobber a great
blue heron, strangle a chukar, pillage the cooler of a ran-
dom river runner, or bag a Rocky Mountain bighorn
sheep, replacement to native desert bighorns wiped out
decades ago by overhunting and domestic livestock dis-
eases. Supplement this diet with wild onion, yucca pods,
and the fruit of the prickly pear cactus. I could go fishing.

While the Fremont fished native squawfish, I would catch introduced species—carp, catfish, and other exotics that have since overtaken native river habitat. This eclectic ecology affects the purity of tonight's menu. My husband and I will eat like the Fremont, with adjustments. Pockets full of plump, pungent juniper berries, I return to camp.

The menu is roast lamb, the closest legal meat to a bighorn sheep, baked with juniper sauce in a very un-Fremontlike cast-iron Dutch oven, fresh corn roasted in the husk then eaten with dashes of cumin and squeezes of lime, and *posole* with black beans and *chipotle* peppers. I stuff the leg of lamb according to a recipe rehearsed on a different ranger patrol. On that river trip we discovered that we had no string to bind the roast. Since the nearest town was a sixty-mile death march from our camp, we searched our gear for a string substitute. Duct tape? Nylon webbing boat straps? The cable on the come-along the ranger uses to peel flipped rafts off boulders? We tied the roast with dental floss.

Tonight's *posole* simmers while the grill awaits the corn. The roast bakes under a crown of bright cotton-wood embers, double-stacked with a second Dutch oven of peach pie. We pop the wine cork, turn the gnats and mosquitoes over to the bats, and watch this gorgeous river flow by. Is this living by the Creed?

The gourmet fetishism of the 1980s turned us into

food snobs. There is nothing new about this condition—diet has had a centuries-long relation to class and status—except its irony. Organ meats, edible flowers, blood sausage, and the like, once the fare of peasants, now sizzle the palates of the affluent, who scorn cheap mainstream bologna; PAM; SPAM; anything pink, puffy, or partially hydrogenated; and other foods containing the oil-based flavors we fought Iraq for. The food elite have adopted the cuisine of the poor. But they have left the poor with the ketchup bottle.

To irony add the illusion that we *can* live off the land or eat food close to the source. Not too many people remember what the source is. Not much of either the source or the land is left. Imagine everyone in Newark foraging. Imagine yourself wringing the necks of chickens or grappling with bleeding, bleating goats.

Behind the excesses the foodies launched an awareness of food politics and the relation between diet—what we eat, how it is grown, the resources consumed to produce it—and individual and planetary health. A diet less dependent on the mass-food apparatus also may require an apocalyptic eradication of food taboos. To pull us back from the ecocidal brink, writes Calvin Schwabe in *Unmentionable Cuisine*, we must put more songbird, reptile, roadkill, rodent, dog, cat, tongue, brain, and gonad—that is, fresh ingredients, locally procured—on our tables.

It may not be possible to eat like a Fremont, but their

adaptability, resourcefulness, and intimate knowledge of this harsh desert environment are instructive. Surrounding me, in fact, lies the ultimate "from scratch" cuisine. Carp ceviche and raven confit. Jerked kit fox. Tanagers *en croûte*. Bunny fajitas. Lopped-off haunch of feral cow or the nearest Labrador retriever. Eat your pets!

RIPARIAN ROAST

Remove the excess fat from a leg of lamb and throw the fat to the catfish. Rub the outside of the meat with olive oil, the inside with salt and pepper, then stuff it with garlic cloves and a thatch of cilantro. Tie the meat with dental floss—unflavored, unwaxed. Crush a few tablespoons of juniper berries in your fingers. If you are not employed by the federal government, take off your clothes, rub your juniper-scented fingertips all over your body, and flit about on the beach. Pour an inch or so of red wine into a Dutch oven; add the juniper berries and meat. Cook with embers below and on the lid, replenishing embers as needed. When the meat is done, dispose of the fat in an environmentally appropriate manner. The sauce: Add more wine, some water or stock, and stir, scraping bits off the bottom of the pot. Simmer until reduced.

LORRIE MOORE

Chop Suey Xmas

1996: Oy. The holidays with our two-year-old boy who
has scarcely recovered from Halloween—its "mean punk-
ins" and election-year Bob Dole masks ringing the front
bell. Nine November nightmares: "There's a scary man in
my room," our two-year-old cries, dashing into ours.

"A scary man?"

"Yeah. Bob Dole!"

"Bob, go home! There. Now let's get back to sleep."

Mostly he does. And soon, once again, it is only Mis-
ter McGregor from "Petey Rat" and occasionally "Humpy
Dumpy" who give him a fright. But by this time it is well
into December. The mall and municipal Christmas tinsel

have been up so long we no longer notice it. Now, despite our anticeremonialist leanings, it is time to do something commemorative at home—we are, after all, creating memories for our child. There is a possibility that, at two, he will remember this as his first "holiday season" (at a theological loss, we have adopted the retail phrase). We must scramble.

Performance anxiety pervades the household. We have to do all the holidays, if we do any. Hanukkah for my husband, Kwanza for my son, and, of course, Christmas (I think, in my gentile-centric way) for everyone. There is a ragtag, castaway quality to our family that holidays seem to underscore. Our family is a desperate improvisation. Our family is a strange, Nietzschean rendition of *Gilligan's Island*. As was, perhaps, the family of my childhood, where, with various Hindu students, we also sometimes celebrated a kind of ad hoc *divali*.

"Do we have to do Kwanza? It's really just an invention," says my husband.

"Unlike the others?"

"It's artificial."

"Unlike Santa Claus, who is, of course, so natural? Practically organic, practically *vegan*—coming down a chimney like that!"

I own a book on Kwanza, but have not had time to read it, not really. I have opened it, spotted a lot of illustrations of crafts items to make at home, then shut it in a

sweat. I need more help with this. I cannot do it alone. I cannot even see the words "needlepoint wall hanging" without feeling inadequate and faint. My husband's holiday indifference now starts to seem like laziness. He hasn't a clue when Hanukkah begins this year. He cannot exactly say, when I ask, what a Maccabee even is. He is a nice Jewish boy but not a good Jewish boy. (If he were a good Jewish boy, why would he have married me?)

Now I find myself saying loudly, "Why does the shiksa have to get out the menorah every year? Why does the shiksa always have to light the candles? Why must the shiksa be the one to teach your child the dreidel song?"

All our two-year-old wants out of the holidays is a very specific present: gum. It is the thing he has wanted for almost six months now and has been denied. He spotted some once in the mouth of a baby-sitter, and has since then staged his own toddler version of a radio pledge drive: *"Gum, gum, gum!"* He studies my mouth for telltale movements—ironic moues and snaps, chompings, and pursings. If I bite my marital tongue, or if I have my marital tongue in my (marital) cheek, he says hopefully, "Mommy, what's in your mouth? You have gum?" He is on the lookout for deviously disguised content. He is on the lookout for cud.

This year, for the holidays to work at all, for festive food and presents for the relatives, we are going to have to rely on all those mail-order catalogs we already threw out.

Oops. We send poinsettias from the corner florist instead. We get a slightly dehydrated Christmas tree, park it close to a radiator, and decorate it in a kind of crazed, slapdash way (tinfoil, string, Christmas cards). The next morning all the needles drop—in a long continuous *whoosh* like rain. The tree now resembles a giant TV antenna—one littered with debris from a windstorm. We vacuum for hours.

On Christmas Eve we build a fire, then snuff it out with an old wet towel, realizing, fearfully, that we haven't cleaned the flue in years. (We are still reeling from parenthood; our last normal year was 1993.) The boiler crashes. We plug in the space heaters. We order take-out Chinese. It is only then, when almost all is lost and I am feeling so unexpectedly sad, that I realize deep down what a sucker I am for the beautiful fake Christmas German-American commerce concocted for us years ago. A boon for the economy and a pernicious sweet for the mind. But it moves me. My heart is a chump. I actually *like* the shopping and the gift wrap and the carols—even the smiling, tinkling store music. I like the invented holiday miracles—at least as they are portrayed on the TV specials!— the unexpected kindnesses and transformations. And looking out the window and seeing only sleet, I realize I even like the snow. Where, now, is that lovely perfect Christmas? On whose open fire are those goddamn chestnuts roasting? I have a fiction writer's weakness for fiction. It is an occupational hazard. A business thing.

"Well," I say, spooning out chop suey. Can I spoon out enough cheer as well? "Merry Christmas, you guys! Merry, merry Christmas!"

Our two-year-old is watching my lips and jaw. His eyebrows lift and his eyes grow knowing and bright. "Mommy?" he says. "You have gum?"

Bitter Honey Cake

My father's assistant, Nenad, used to tell me stories while hammering nails into the wood to pinch the leather so no water could leak into the clogs. The hammer punctuated his stories like a *gusle*, the one-stringed Balkan fiddle, but more sharply, less melodiously.

Nenad told me about Prince Marko, who sucked his mother's breasts for seven years, and for seven more ate nothing but honey. Marko could squeeze water out of a log dried for nine years. His horse could jump the length of nine lances and the height of three. On hot summer days a hawk in the sky shaded him with his wings. Marko slew Musa Kesejiya, in whose breast, beneath three rib

cages, were three hearts—the first working, the second
dancing, and the third nesting a sleeping snake. When the
snake awoke, the dead Musa leaped over the barren land.

In 1989, twenty years after Nenad had told me his
stories, I went back to find him at the Weeping Willow,
the village in Croatia where he now worked as a clog-
maker on his own. Where once horses plowed the fields
along a dirt road, tractors oozed green oil puddles along a
paved highway. A cracked wooden shoe still hung from a
pole on Nenad's whitewashed house to advertise his trade.

My entry startled Nenad. He stopped working—pil-
ing wooden soles—and laughed for joy, and then shook
his head sadly. "Eh, my *yozzo*, seven years have come and
gone since we saw each other last!"

After an hour of Nenad's talking, I interrupted him,
"You are such a good talker. Do you mind if I record
you?" From my shirt pocket I pulled out a microcassette
recorder I had bought in an electronic store in New York's
Chinatown.

Nenad's clear eyes looked at the cassette recorder as if
it were a time bomb. His forehead showed its new creases,
his graying eyebrows made tall arches, and he didn't talk
until I turned off the machine.

"Nenad, where did you learn how to tell tales? At the
hearth, on your grandfather's knee?"

"I went to the library, read them, and told them as I re-

membered them." A myth fell apart right before my very ears. "Of course," he said, "I added a thing here and there."

"But I . . . I believed you to be an epic storyteller raised by the spoken word!"

"After every story you said, 'More! More!' So what could I do? I went to the library on lunch breaks to find more." He opened his calloused hands as if to show me that he hid no weapons in them.

I had thought that, instead of going through a writing workshop back in the States, I would simply listen to him for a couple of days and nights and find the formula for triggering a wellspring of storytelling in me, from our common ground. And now this. "Still, who taught you how to tell stories?"

"No. Why are you so stuck on this? It's easy to tell a story; what's the big deal? You have to start from somewhere right here, and lead the listener further and further away, or start from far away and get us here."

"It's easy to say, but do it!"

"Well, you have the beer mug in your hand. You give yourself a bit of time and go, 'A long time ago there was a beer mug, and it lived in a tavern. Of course, it was not the only mug living there. It lived with its twenty-three siblings. And many a dry lip . . .'—and off we go, see!"

"But, how would you continue it?"

"All right, I'll tell you as we pick plums," he said.

"Would you like to help me gather our plums? Last night the wind shook them off the trees."

In his orchard I put more plums into my mouth than into the basket because they tasted like pineapples. The air was so clear—a powerful wind had blown the night before—that I could see, to the south, above an indented and mossy red roof, a funeral procession with a horse-pulled hearse snaking its way up a dirt road. Beyond it, some fifty miles away, the blue mountains of Bosnia lay flattened like wet shirts on a drying line.

"You are looking at my childhood home," Nenad said. "I'm amazed that the roof hasn't caved in yet. At the beginning of the war the Germans barged into that house, seized my father and grandfather from the dinner table, and shot them to death against the barn. Several years later half a dozen Germans walked into our yard and I had no time to run and hide in the woods, so I hid in bed and shivered under a thick goose-down cover.

"A pair of boots stamped over the floorboards toward me louder and louder. The cover was pulled off and a huge soldier loomed over me. An 'Agkhh' broke out of my throat, my eyes bulged. The German lowered his hand— I thought to strangle me.

"Instead, he placed his cold palm on my forehead and held it there. Then he poured a glass of water from the bucket that was on the chair in the kitchen, put some white pills into the water, crushed them with a spoon, and

pressed my lips with the edge of the glass against my teeth. I could hardly swallow. The liquid was shudderingly bitter—I thought it was poison. I would keel over and die.

"He took a paper sack out of his black leather bag—I guess he was a military doctor—and out of it a honey cake. Where he'd got it I'll never know, but I am sure he hadn't baked it himself. He gave it to me and I have never chewed anything sweeter before or since.

"He looked sternly at my mouth as if to make sure I was chewing. When I finished, he handed me another, and I chewed it slowly, savoring its honey. After swallowing the last of it, I wanted more, but didn't dare to ask him with my voice or my hands. My eyes shifted in the direction of the paper sack.

"The German raised his forefinger and shook it sideways in front of my aching eyes and said, 'Nein!' That was the only word spoken between us. He stood up and walked into the yard, his boots crunching gravel, less and less. He shouted something to the soldiers, and they all marched away, raising a screen of dust.

"Eh, my brother, you can't imagine how I felt right then. First he—for me it was the same German—kills my father, and then gives me the sweetest cakes I could ever have!"

He's an unstoppable storyteller, I thought. *Instead of a writing program, I need a war. If I survive I'll have enough stories to last me a lifetime.*

After we'd gathered several basketfuls of plums we sat outside his workshop. Nenad took off his cap and put it over his knee.

Nenad's tabby jumped, grabbed the rim of his cap, and tried to pull it out of his hands. Nenad scratched the cat on the head and said, "My dear kitty." He patted her more tenderly than I had ever seen a man his age do, and he talked.

"One night the Germans entered the village and were about to round up thirty or forty people. They planned to kill them because the partisans had killed three or four German soldiers in the woods nearby. But the soldiers first axed some chickens to cook quietly at a secluded house in an apple orchard where nobody from the village could see them. There were some black cats there, and no black cats ever came to our end of the village. So when I saw a black cat running down the road with a bloody rooster's head in its mouth, I screamed, 'The Germans are coming!' We ran into the woods and listened to the echoing of shotguns. The Germans killed ten, but most of the people in the village were saved—by the black cat!" He picked up his tabby, who looked like a camouflaged paratrooper.

Blue sheets of lightning shivered in the east. "But it's getting late," said Nenad, "and you don't want to miss your train, do you?" As I walked to the train station, the leaves in the woods—the tongues of the wind—mur-

mured. The stones on the shoulder of the road crunched beneath my feet and told me how Jesus was tempted in the desert to make bread out of stones and how instead he later made wine out of water.

The stones told me how vicious armies and the good people had passed. And I thought: If the stones can tell stories, I can, too.

Brain Food

A few days ago, my seven-year-old's face took on a solem-
nity that one normally sees in a veterinarian confronted with
a case of mad cow disease. I knew an important question
was coming—perhaps about God, the source of babies, or
whether a warlock or a wizard had more power. The last
time he got this serious, he wanted to know if Buddhists
were those people who ran around with no clothes on.

"Dad," he said. "If you eat someone's brain, will you
get as smart as them?"

"I don't think so."

"How do you know?"

There I was, trapped as usual by the logic of a child. If

I didn't know the answer, then I was obviously someone who could benefit from eating the brain of a genius. And if I did know the answer—how the hell did I find out?

"Look at it this way," I said. "If you ate someone's brain who was dumber than you, would you get dumb?"

He thought for a moment and said no.

I congratulated myself on once again doing my bit to maintain the gross lie of childhood—that adults possess a superior intellect. It didn't occur to me until later that this might make me a likely candidate for a meal.

I went into the living room where he was constructing a city of Legos.

"Hey," I said. "Do you have somebody in mind?"

"For what?"

"You know. Somebody's brain to eat."

"Like who?"

"Like me."

"No," he said.

As I watched him play, I began to think about whose brain I would eat if the chance came along. It was a lot easier to figure out whose brain I'd pass on. There were plenty of people a ton smarter than me, but I wasn't interested in inheriting their mental foibles as well. Ultimately I realized that if someone was stupid enough to let their brain get eaten, I wouldn't want to eat it.

As I pondered this further I realized that I have, in fact, eaten brain on at least two occasions. Here in Montana

there is an all-night café that serves calf brains and eggs, eaten primarily by drunken cowboys and college kids after the bars have closed. Most people dump condiments on the meal until nothing is visible but mustard, ketchup, hot sauce, or all three, with extra pepper. There is something unsavory about the idea of eating brains. It must be concealed even from the self. Unfortunately, there is no secret way to eat them here. When you order brains and eggs, the waitress yells across the room to the line cook, "He needs them." Everyone in the joint then knows some dope is trying to get smart.

One night I was that dope. The brains looked like gray grits and tasted like tofu. The next day I felt dumb as a cow.

As a native of eastern Kentucky, I have naturally eaten squirrel brains, which is considered a delicacy on par with beaver tail or buffalo hump in Montana. The problem with squirrel brains is the same problem with eating the rest of the squirrel—it takes a lot to fill you up. And who wants to gorge on the appetizer, when a fine entrée of possum stew is yet to come? Incidentally, the brain of a possum is one I won't eat. I draw the line at marsupials.

If it were possible to get something out of eating a human brain, I'd probably opt for artists, writers, and scientists. I'd skip anyone with drastic problems, such as van Gogh, Poe, or people from Idaho. The correct strategy is to try and improve one's known shortcomings. If

you have trouble with right from wrong, go for Socrates. If you're scared of the dark, eat a blind man's brain. I've always been weak at math, and the brain of one of the great mathematicians might do me some good. I could then balance a checkbook, set the clock on the VCR, and figure out gas mileage. Maybe I'd suddenly know how many acres of soy Farmer Brown harvested on that damn SAT test all those years ago.

Due to my experience with brain-eating, I believe I'd grind it to a paste, throw it in a blender with cinnamon and honey, and make a milk shake. Drinking it would be a grave ritual performed with utmost care and respect. I'd light candles, sit cross-legged, and offer a toast: "Here's looking at Euclid."

I broke my reverie to ask my son if he was still worrying about getting smarter. He didn't look at me as he pressed Legos together.

"No," he said. "Are you worried I want to eat your brain?"

"Not at all."

"Good," he said. "I don't think it's worth it."

I looked at him for a long time. He's already more adept at a computer than I am. He can name the dinosaurs from a variety of eras and sometimes he beats me at chess. He even plays the piano. Now he understands that my brain's not worth eating. I wonder how he got so smart on a diet of pizza and frosted flakes.

STEWART O'NAN

Tots

When I was in high school I got a job washing dishes at a synagogue, for the caterer there. This was in Pittsburgh, in Squirrel Hill, 1976. I was in a garage band and our bassist, Marty Roth, worked there, so he got us all jobs—me, Mark Gaudio (our guitarist), and our drummer, Mark Serotta.

I'd had jobs before, painting and stuff, but nothing where you had your own time card and got a check every other week. We all started at two dollars an hour. Marty was already up to two seventy-five; this seemed like another tax bracket to us. And Marty worked a lot of hours. He had a Sun bass cabinet and a Nakamichi tape deck, which none of us had ever heard of.

He'd call up and say, "Goat,"—my nickname then—
"you wanna work this weekend?" And I'd say yeah or no,
depending on whether I could convince my girlfriend to
go out or not. Her name was Merle, and she was my first
serious girlfriend. Her parents drove a Lancia and hated
me because I wasn't Jewish. It was very Romeo and Juliet
for a few weeks.

I worked a lot that winter. I remember getting up be-
fore it was light and walking through the snow in my blue
Pumas, the suede ones that bled on your socks. The first
thing you'd do was punch in, then hang your coat up and
tie on an apron.

The apron represented all kinds of things. At first we
were embarrassed by it, being teenaged boys. For a while
it was simply a reminder of what a crappy job we had, but
then we began to wear it like a uniform, sloppily but with
affected pride. We were kitchen—not cooks and definitely
not the guy who ran the place (Jerry Myers, a great
blowhard of a boss, not above reducing a waitress to tears).
In spirit, we were closest to the waitresses. We worked, we
didn't sit around on our asses like Michael the cook, and
we got paid shit and nobody cared about us. We were
proud of that.

Once you got the apron on, it was time to do some
heavy prep. If it was the men's club brunch, you were talk-
ing whitefish and lox, trays and trays of it. Someone had to
cut the bagels, maybe two hundred of them. And woe to

the dude who got stuck with fruit cup. After ten minutes, the melon baller would have you shaking your wrist like a hit batter.

"Where the fuck are my relish bowls?" Jerry would come in screaming. "You, Mergatroid, O'Neill, get ya thumb outta ya ass." And you'd have to run into the store-room for a five gallon jug of baby corn, your fingertips numb from arranging the celery and gherkins in the crushed ice.

Dinner meant stirring the vat of beef barley soup— slop it on yourself and it would burn through your jeans— washing several crates worth of lettuce, cutting pans and pans of kugel, splitting and then breading four hundred breasts of chicken. And then there were those special tasks Marty had to initiate you into: edging the plate with a garnish of whipped sweet potato, squeezing the pastry bag so hard that your knuckles ached the next morning; molding a pile of cold chopped liver into the shape of a leaping salmon, a black olive for its eye; and, best of all, operating that mysterious black lake of bubbling grease known as the Frialator.

The bread was already out there, and the butter, the salad, and salad dressing (in a metal three-cup lazy Susan whose edges never failed to draw blood). There was a lull of a few minutes, but we weren't allowed to go out on the dock for a butt, or better, to get stoned. We invented reasons to go down the sloping ramp to the basement, where

the walk-in fridge and freezer were. There were boxes
piled along the walls, stacks of folding chairs, a dolly you
could pile racks of dishes on, a barrel of Zep cleaner with
a spout. The temptation to go out on the dock was
painful, but someone might see you from the parking lot.
Just take a toke behind the walk-in, hope Jerry doesn't
come downstairs. Bring something up, make it look good.

Now the salad dishes were coming back in, the wait-
resses hefting bus boxes on their shoulders. Mark Gaudio
manned the Insinkerator, shoving the food down into the
funnel of the opening, the machine growling as it tore it
to bits. Every so often a waitress wouldn't take all the sil-
ver out of her box, and a fork would ring and chatter on
the blades, maybe even jump out if you didn't clap a plate
over the opening. Mark Serotta rinsed and racked, sliding
heavy plastic trays into the front of the big, swishing Ho-
bart, while I worked the Ass, pulling out the burning, dry
dishes and stacking them on a dolly. When you finished
emptying a tray, you turned it vertical, stuck it in a gutter
that ran behind the Hobart, and slid it back to the front as
hard as you could, hoping the spray might get someone.

Salad wasn't bad, especially if your Ass was fast. The
guys on front would come back when they were done and
help shelve.

Between courses the waitresses took a break in their
room just off the kitchen, and then, when the roast was
done, or whatever the main course was, Michael the cook

would put down his cigarette and, with the disdain of a famous conductor, he would serve. The waitresses came in with their trays and banged out through the swinging doors. When they came back, everything was quiet. Michael was outside on the side porch smoking, his job pretty much done.

This was the best time of the night, because there were no dishes coming in and you got to eat, too—and for free, which impressed us at first. You could slug down as much Coke as you wanted. You could have anything.

But after working with the food all afternoon long, you didn't want any of it. It was under your nails and crusted on your arms. You'd seen it dropped on the floor and picked up again, you'd seen it last week in the walk-in, and maybe the week before. What you wanted was something clean and untouched, something you could trust. What you wanted was Tater Tots.

"We got Tots," Marty said. "How many you guys want Tots?"

He tore open the bag and dumped them in the Frialator, and in minutes they rose again, gleaming in the dripping steel basket. "Tots, baby."

You'd get enough ketchup for everyone and open a new Coke and follow everyone down the ramp with your bowlful and sit among the boxes and dollies, eating. Maybe one of the waitresses would come down, the ones who liked you—Roz or Cathy—and they'd ask you outside to smoke

a joint or just stand there bitching about Jerry or their boyfriends. They'd ask what the band was up to, and Marty would tell them; the rest of us were too shy. You'd eat all the Tots, just like you cleaned your plate at home, because you were astonished by how much food went to waste here—gone rotten, left on the plate, or just tossed.

And then it was time to work. You could count on being here till 1:00, 1:30, mopping the floor while Michael, who hadn't done anything since main course, sat on his ass, bitching because he had to stay to lock up. You did the water glasses and silverware last, the fake corkboard trays. Dry it off, put it away.

You untied your apron and noticed your jeans were wet where it stopped. You counted the hours so far this week and projected the rest, multiplied them by two and thought of what records you'd buy at Jim's—The Ramones and maybe an old Stooges boot you'd had your eye on. And then, with all the lights but the one by the phone off, you'd punch out and head down the long ramp and let yourself out onto the loading dock. It was snowing hard and no one had a car, so you popped the bottle of kosher champagne you'd hidden in with the case of empties and you all walked home down the middle of Shady Avenue, passing the bottle between the four of you. In the cold, your hands still felt greasy, and you knew you had to take a shower when you got home, even though all you wanted was to fall in bed, never move again.

"Anyone got a butt?" Mark Serotta said.

You did and he lit it.

"This thing's killed," Marty said, and tossed the bottle in a snow bank so it disappeared.

The snow fell so slow.

"Are we gonna practice tomorrow?"

And Mark Gaudio would say, "What are you, stupid—we're all working breakfast tomorrow."

"Oh yeah," you'd say. "I forgot."

Pork

My grandmother was famous for her desserts, especially her strawberry shortcake. She made wonderful moist, crumbly biscuits from scratch, topped with strawberries and fresh cream she whipped up with a hand mixer, gritty with sugar. She'd remove the biscuits from the oven and leave them on top of the stove, covered with a clean dishtowel, to cool and to teach my grandfather and me patience and restraint. Eventually, when her hands became arthritic, she had to give up making the shortcake, her signature dessert, except on special occasions. By the time she turned seventy—she lived deep into her eighties— each of her thin fingers went in several different directions

and her knuckles looked like someone had sewn quarters beneath the skin. Still, if I came home for a visit—say, to paint one side of the house or to introduce her to a new grandchild—she put those twisted knuckles to work kneading flour into biscuits, after which she retired to her bedroom and closed the door, to abide the throbbing pain in private. It's love that makes good cooks.

Fear, as a culinary motivator, doesn't work nearly so well. My grandmother feared meat long before it became fashionable. A product of her time, her anxiety had nothing to do with cholesterol, fat, or clogged arteries. Nor was she sentimental about animals. Having endured the depression, it wouldn't have occurred to my grandmother to concern herself with "quality of life" issues for barnyard fowl. She'd spent too much of her life worrying about whether there would be enough money for a roasting chicken on Sunday to concern herself with whether the bird in question had ranged free before it entered her range. No, her concern was for us, for our safety. Under-cooked meat could kill you, she reminded us, an observation that to me always seemed tinged with morality. Animals were beasts, in my grandmother's view, and whenever the word "beast" required an adjective, she supplied one: filthy. What differentiated filthy beasts from humans was our moral sense. Animals didn't know right from wrong, as a result of which their behavior was disgusting. They wallowed. They rutted. They befouled

themselves. Who knew what germs and bacteria coursed through their bloodstreams? There was only one way to cleanse them and that was in the oven. Put the animal in there. How long? Until you're sure.

Since her objection to meat was as much moral as medical, my grandmother feared all undercooked meats, not just chicken and pork. Like most women of her generation, she cooked all meat into a state of such thorough compliance that gravy was required to supply the lubrication necessary for mastication. My mother and I mocked her with rare steaks and lamb chops, often done outdoors on a grill, a method of cooking that seemed barbaric to my grandmother. The idea of raw flame licking at animal flesh, reducing fat to dripping, hissing, combustible liquid, turning the meat black and sooty on the outside even as it remained cool and bloody on the inside, was too much for her. When I was a teenager, I discovered I could drain all the color out of my grandmother's face by sneaking up behind her, pinching some raw hamburger from beneath its reassuring cellophane, and popping the wad in my mouth. To her way of thinking, such behavior was barely distinguishable from Russian roulette played with real bullets.

Pork was my grandmother's favorite meat despite (because of?) the fact that it was the most dangerous. The threat of trichinosis in undercooked pork was real, of course, and I suspect she enjoyed seeing herself as the

protector of those who sat down at her table. But she also
enjoyed the taste of pork, and so, as a boy, did I. Most
people have forgotten what pork used to taste like before
breeders improved it. Now it's lean and tough and flavor-
less—"the other white meat." Thirty years ago it was a
real killer, true, but it tasted good. I don't think I'm being
nostalgic when I remember tender pork chops, and if I
concentrate, I can still taste the seared, crisp, glistening
fat around the edge of one of those chops fresh from
my grandmother's smoking, buttery frying pan. Her own
personal favorite was sausage, and we had baked sausage
once a week. When the patties entered her oven they
looked like hamburgers. When they emerged, an hour or
ninety minutes later, they looked like something you'd
wedge under a door you wanted to keep open, roughly a
quarter of their original size, nearly submerged now in the
fat that had been cooked out of them, fat that continued to
sputter and spit evilly on top of the stove after she had
transferred the patties to a platter spread with a paper
towel. They were dense and wobbly now, and still greasy
enough to skitter away from the fork. Your best bet was to
pinion them with the tines of your fork and use a good
strong knife. Each sausage patty contained no more than
two bites, but you could chew on them a good long while,
like jerky. Even so, my grandmother wasn't sure she'd
completed the job and she examined not only her own
sausage but also my grandfather's and mine for telltale

pinkness, any indication that the meat might produce first lockjaw, then lingering, agonizing death. "Are they done, Dick?" she asked my grandfather. When he assured her that they were done and then some, she urged him to be honest. It would be no trouble to put them back in the oven. Better to wait another fifteen minutes than for all of us to end up in the hospital, doubled up, waiting to have our stomachs pumped. Because that's what'll happen to you if sausage isn't cooked through, she warned. My grandfather, probably visualizing the agony my grand- mother predicted, always wanted to know how in the world we were supposed to enjoy the food with her talk- ing about getting our stomachs pumped before we could even fill them. By then I was on my fourth sausage. At that age I was not a prey to my grandmother's grisly visions.

I never made any secret of my favorite foods, and be- cause I was a favored child, my grandmother honored my wishes more than she should have. On weeknights I was a constant guest at her table because my mother worked in Schenectady, a full hour away, and didn't get home until six, by which time my grandmother fully intended to have her dinner dishes washed, dried, and returned safely to the kitchen cupboard. If my grandfather minded having the supper menu dictated by a child, he never said so, and in truth he was not the sort of man who took much pleasure in any food that preceded dessert. He claimed to love mashed potatoes, and we had them at every meal, but life

had taught my grandfather to love what he could afford and to disdain whatever was beyond his reach. I grew up thinking that what we called Spanish peanuts, the kind with the red skins, were the most delicious and desirable variety of nut, and I always worried, when my grandfather and I walked downtown to an ice cream shop that for some reason sold bulk nuts warmed under hot lights and served up in small paper sleeves, that they'd be out of the red ones, my grandfather's favorites, and we'd be forced to make do with some lesser variety, like cashews, which I'd never tasted but knew to be inferior. But as long as there were mashed potatoes, he appeared not to care what meat my grandmother served at supper, so I mostly got my way, except during Lent, when God got His way and we ate fish sticks.

I was an adolescent before it began to dawn on me that there might be a downside to my grandmother's treating my wishes with such deference. What I'd counted on as a boy of six—that she'd never forget what my favorite foods were—I came to see as a curse by the time I was sixteen and my tastes began to change. I remember as a teenager trying to tell my grandmother that I didn't like cherry pie anymore. "Don't be silly," she replied. "You've *always* loved cherry pie." Ignoring a warning look from my grandfather, I attempted to explain that, without meaning to, I'd lost my taste for it, that the cloying texture and sweetness I'd craved as a child provoked an entirely differ-

ent response in me now. "People change," I ventured philosophically, only vaguely aware that I was challenging a whole belief system, for it was my grandmother's own conviction that people didn't change, not really, and it unnerved her to consider that I'd come to the opposite conclusion about something so fundamental. When I told her that people changed, she regarded me as if I might be an impostor tricked out to resemble the boy she knew, the boy who loved cherry pie, the boy, it seemed clear, she preferred. Which was why, years later, we never had the talk I wanted to have had about spareribs.

As a boy, I loved spareribs, perhaps because we didn't have them very often. Ribs are, after all, mostly bone, and my grandmother was too thrifty to purchase bones except when bones were on special. I think the first year I went away to college my grandmother must have missed me terribly, because when I returned home that summer to work road construction with my father, she had all my favorite foods waiting for me, including spareribs. "Your favorites," she said, rather pointedly, as if she feared I might reiterate my belief that "people change." Probably she was trying to convince herself that *I* hadn't changed, despite the fact that I'd returned home with long hair and enough high-handed moral certainty to be in step with the times.

My grandmother's recipe for spareribs was simple. Coat rack of ribs with brown sugar, cover with a large can of Hunt's tomato sauce, and place in a preheated oven at

450 degrees. Ignore for three hours. She liked to cook ribs on Saturday morning, then serve them at the noon meal which, as my grandmother aged, began to creep by small increments into morning. That first summer I returned from college "the noon meal" was served closer to 11:30, though my grandmother always maintained that this was a mistake, that things had gotten done sooner than she expected, a fiction she didn't really expect anyone to believe, so long as we didn't challenge her right to maintain it. From the time I was a boy, she had timed all of her meals right to the minute. My grandfather got off work at the glove shop at five in the afternoon. If he didn't dawdle, it took him six minutes to walk home. At 5:07 the steaming casserole came out of the oven, whether he had arrived or not.

So. In order for the spareribs to be served at 11:30 on Saturday morning they had to enter the oven at 8:30. By 9:00 the smell of pork fat being reduced to shimmering liquid began to seep under the door of the spare bedroom I occupied during the summer. In 1968 the legal drinking age in New York was eighteen, and that's what I was. Along with my old high-school pals, also returned from college for the summer, I felt a profound obligation to do whatever was legal. At the very least. I often worked fifty hours a week or more, and my reward for so much back-breaking labor was a paycheck that, wisely saved and carefully monitored, would get me through another year at the

University of Arizona and keep me in cheap beer during June, July, and August in dingy local bars. We were paid on Fridays and so it was on Friday nights that our carousing was most purposeful and sustained. My grandmother disapproved of the idea of my coming home drunk after the bars closed, but I was a legal adult and I was doing well at the university and I was full of my youth, and so she held her tongue and cooked ribs.

By ten o'clock on Saturday morning, sleeping with my mouth open, fighting off wave after wave of vivid alcohol-induced nightmares, I could begin to taste pork grease on my hairy tongue, and sometimes the cooking ribs would insinuate their way into my dream narratives the way collapsed sinuses can sometimes induce dreams of strangulation. Often, half awake, I would roll over, trying to face away from the pork, a maneuver that caused my head to pound and a wave of stale beer nausea to creep up my gullet. Unable to sleep and unwilling to wake, I'd conclude that I'd forgotten to open the bedroom window the night before, and I'd dream over and over that I was getting out of bed, throwing the window wide open, and gulping the pure morning air like cold water from a mountain stream.

At 11:15 I'd hear my grandmother setting the table in the kitchen, talking softly with my grandfather about what time I'd gotten in and about the drunken laughter that had spilled out of the car and into the quiet street when I

was deposited on the front steps at 2:00 A.M. At 11:25 I'd sit up on the edge of the bed, plant my feet on the floor and test it for movement. At 11:30 my grandmother would knock gently and summon me to the table where the rack of spareribs sat steaming, shrunken, their bones no longer adhering in their sockets but glistening brightly in the hot, noonday sun that streamed relentlessly in the kitchen window. My grandmother's spareribs were, of course, exactly what I deserved, and she watched me eat them to make sure I understood what they meant.

I did. I understood well. My grandmother's profound belief that life was not to be enjoyed too much, that pleasure must always partake of pain, that the world is bigger than we who inhabit it, that it holds us in no particular regard, that what we enjoy too completely may in the end prove our undoing. And that nothing, nothing, nothing ever comes to us simple and clean, not even love.

Lady Food

Progress is not my thing. I don't have a microwave, for instance. I drive a car until it has two hundred thousand miles on it, and I write books in longhand, on a legal pad. But even I have to admit that American food has dramatically improved in recent years. You can find good bread almost everywhere. You can buy good lettuce, though you still have to grow your own tomatoes. Fancy restaurant food has moved from ubiquitous steak and baked potato to include, well . . . everything. Food is healthier and more innovative than ever before.

Still, I often find my Luddite streak kicking in when I am presented with a menu as long as a novella, offering

rhapsodic descriptions of something like "fresh grilled newly dug tiny potatoes served on a bed of roasted corn-bacon relish and collards *frisés*." I don't like the way they put the sauce *under* the food either, instead of on top of it; and frankly, I'd love to have a cocktail with one of those little paper umbrellas in it.

My first idea of an elegant meal came from my mother, whose bridge club met every Thursday at noon for lunch and bridge, rotating houses, for years and years until its members began to die or move to Florida. I loved the cut flowers, the silver, the pink cloths on the tables. The food my mama gave the bridge club was wonderful, though it was very clear to me even then that the way these ladies were was a way I'd never be. They feasted upon molded pink salad that melted on the tongue (back then I thought *all* salads were Jell-O salads); a canned asparagus / Velveeta cheese soufflé; and something called Chicken Crunch that involved mushroom soup, chicken, Chinese noodles, pecans, and Lord knows what else. All of Mama's bridge lunch recipes required gelatin or mushroom soup or pecans. This was Lady Food.

When my mother died a few years ago I inherited her recipe box. I sat down and read it like a novel—for in fact, our recipes tell everything about us: where we live, what we value, how we spend our time. My mother made all her own bread, for instance. Her recipe for Salvation Cake had a Bible verse listed beside each ingredient (the almonds came

from Genesis 43:11), and the only instruction given for baking was the cryptic Proverbs 23:14. Fat content was *not* a consideration. Biscuits called for lard, and Chocolate Velvet Cake required one cup of mayonnaise. A hearty beef-and-cheese casserole was named "Husband's Delight."

Then I realized that I, too, have written out my life in recipes. As a young bride I had eleven dessert recipes featuring Cool Whip as the main ingredient. Then came the hibachi and fondue period, then the quiche and crepes phase, and now it's these salsa years. Just this past Christmas I made cranberry salsa for everybody.

My mother would not have touched salsa—let alone sushi!—with a ten-foot pole. She would not have recognized a Portobello mushroom. I think I'll make some biscuits right now, in her memory, if I can just find some lard. One thing she used to say is, "No matter what is wrong with you, a sausage biscuit will make you feel a whole lot better."

Chicken Crunch

½ cup chicken broth

2 cans mushroom soup

3 cups cut-up chicken

1 (7 oz.) can tuna

¼ cup minced onion

1 cup diced celery

1 can mushrooms (optional)

 1 (5 oz.) can water chestnuts, sliced
 1 (3 oz.) can Chinese noodles
 ½ cup almonds

Blend broth and soup into two-quart casserole. Mix other ingredients except almonds. Bake 40 minutes at 350° and add almonds the last few minutes on top.

P.S. I usually use chicken breasts. Four whole ones will be enough to serve eight.

SALVATION CAKE

 1 cup butter (Judges 5:25)
 3½ cups flour (I Kings 4:22)
 3 cups sugar (Jeremiah 6:20)
 2 cups raisins (I Samuel 30:12)
 2 cups figs (I Samuel 30:12)
 1 cup water (Genesis 24:17)
 1 cup almonds (Genesis 43:11)
 6 eggs (Isaiah 10:14)
 1 tsp. honey (Exodus 16:31)
 pinch of salt (Leviticus 2:13)
 2 tsp. baking powder (I Corinthians 5:6)
 spice to taste (I Kings 10:10)

Follow Solomon's advice for making good boys and girls and you will have a good cake (Proverbs 23:14).

Grandma's Table

At one time my grandmother was a legendary cook. She excelled at a kind of country cooking that you will no longer find much of in the Mississippi Delta, where I grew up. You will no longer find much of it because these days, more often than not, Deltans cook out of boxes. They make cakes the way everybody else does, from Duncan Hines containers, and they make their corn bread from prepackaged mixes. If they remain resistant to canned biscuits, they have to come to terms with Bisquick. Frozen vegetables, they have learned, cook nicely in microwave ovens. So does bacon. Soup does, too.

But when I was growing up, in the late '50s and early

'60s, country people made their cakes and breads and biscuits from scratch. They created their own sauces and gravies, seasoning them to taste, and the vegetables they ate came from their gardens. They made their own sausage. The chickens they fried had, until lately, been their neighbors.

Grandma scrambled eggs for me for breakfast, then she tore a couple of fluffy biscuits into bite-size bits and mixed them in with the eggs. If I asked her to, she would fry me up three or four slices of bacon—and the bacon, by the way, had come from our hogs. Sometimes for a change she gave me biscuits with a jar of her homemade molasses. The molasses was dark brown and it was so thick that when you stuck a spoon into it you had a hard time getting the spoon back out, almost as if it were trapped in a pool of quicksand.

Grandma was, at that time, an energetic, hardworking woman. Though blind in one eye from a childhood accident, she was the one who jumped in the pickup truck in the middle of the night to pull cotton trailers to the gin. When the farmhands chopped cotton in June and July, she was out in the field with them, leading the way. She worked her own garden, cleaned the house, and cooked, and for a few years, in the late '50s, took care of her bedridden mother.

If she was troubled by the harshness of the life she'd known, she seldom let on. Yet she had raised my mother

during the Great Depression, and I knew from my grandfather, who talked about such things, that the family had almost starved. The WPA saved them. He got a job helping to build the Yazoo County Courthouse. Between the small amount he made there and Grandma's ability to create meals out of vegetables and fatback, the family survived.

By the time I came along Grandma and Grandpa were living in a house on sixteenth-section land. They owned a television, an old car, and a truck. The house was equipped with running water. There was always plenty to eat—neighbors liked to joke that, at mealtime, the table sagged from all the good food Grandma laid on it. Considering where they had been, she and Grandpa must have felt like they had come a long way. I don't think it's an exaggeration to say that they were both fairly proud of themselves.

At least both of them were until Nick Miller came to stay at their place, at which time Grandma's feelings about food and family, house and hearth, underwent certain changes.

Nick Miller was from Texas. He was from Texarkana, Texas, but if you pointed out that the city of Texarkana was only half Texan, he would puff himself up and tell you, "A little bit of Texas is still a hell of a lot." He pronounced the word Texas just like Ernest Tubb did. *Tex-Us*.

Nick had married my second cousin Lynn, who I always thought was the most beautiful girl I'd ever seen. I remember going down to Gulfport when I was two or three to watch her being crowned homecoming queen at her high school. She wore a long white gown that night, with sequins on it that sparkled under the stadium lights. Her blonde hair seemed to sparkle as well. On the way home that evening I told Grandma that I hoped to marry Lynn.

Naturally enough, I was pissed when I found out about Nick. She'd met him at a dance in Texarkana, where she moved with her mother—my Aunt Lena, who was Grandma's sister—and her father and two younger brothers.

She and Nick came to stay at Grandma's house one weekend in the summer of 1963. Lynn wanted to show him off to all her relatives, so they planned several stops. Because she lived so close to Highway 82, Grandma was the first.

It's been more than thirty years since the afternoon I stood on the porch of my grandparents' house and watched, with the special kind of eagerness that I'm convinced only country kids feel, as Nick and Lynn drove into the yard. They were riding in a long, silver Cadillac. The Cadillac sported Texas license plates. A sticker on the front bumper announced Nick's allegiance to the Dallas Cowboys. He'd played football in college, Grandma had told me, but she was uncertain exactly where.

Chickens scattered, squawking, when the Cadillac pulled in. Nick parked beneath the chinaberry tree, next to the rusty pitcher pump where, for many years, Grandma and Grandpa had drawn their drinking water.

Nick did not cut the engine right away. For a minute or more the Cadillac idled. Through the windshield I could see my new cousin. He had wavy black hair that looked like he'd applied Brylcreem to it, and his chin was big and square. He stared at me, at the porch I was standing on, and at Grandma, who had just walked out the screen door. Then he looked around the yard—at the chickens; at the old section harrow that stood near the road, overgrown by Johnson grass; at the tractor tire in which Grandma had planted a bed of azaleas.

Then he looked at Lynn. He said something to her, and her face, which seconds before had worn a big smile as she waved at me and mouthed the word "*hi*," suddenly went slack. It was as if she'd suffered some massive muscle failure.

"Y'all get out and come in," Grandma hollered. "I just about got supper on the table."

It would help to say a few things about the house that Grandma lived in.

The house had a tin roof and tar-paper siding. Because it was very close to Beaverdam Creek, it flooded from time to time. Grandpa had killed a water moccasin in

their bedroom once, and they were always finding snakeskins in the chest of drawers and the closet.

It wasn't that the house wasn't clean; it was as clean as any house could be, given the fact that it occasionally flooded, that it had the kind of roof that was bound to leak. It was clean, given the fact that it was built two feet off the ground, so that chickens could walk around beneath it and do their business there, as could Grandpa's dog Buster, who was beset by ticks and fleas. But if you lived in a modern ranch-style house in the suburbs, and if you had a maid who came twice a week to clean, Grandma's house left something to be desired.

The room Grandma put Nick and Lynn in was next to the kitchen—between it and Grandma's own bedroom. You had to walk through that room to get from one end of the house to the other. It was the room I slept in when I spent the night with my grandparents—and most nights in the summer I stayed at their house. I remember the room now as the place in which I spent many of my happiest times. I recall the shape of the water stains on the ceiling—one of the stains, Grandpa told me, was shaped exactly like Lake Michigan, and he showed me a map of the Great Lakes to prove it. I remember the way the floor creaked when you put your foot on one particular floorboard in the middle of the room, and I remember how you could hear Buster whimpering beneath you at night when he had a bad dream.

I also remember the conversation that took place between Nick and Lynn in that room the day they arrived. Grandma had led them in there and closed the door so they could get out of their traveling clothes before supper.

Nick's voice was resonant. He was trying to whisper, but he didn't succeed. "I can't do this," he said.

I was in the kitchen helping Grandma. She'd fried up a huge mess of catfish that Grandpa and my father had caught that morning in the Sunflower River. There were homemade hush puppies and a tangy slaw she'd made of shredded cabbage, chopped celery, sweet pickles, and mayonnaise, with a dab of French's mustard thrown in to enhance the flavor.

The kitchen was full of good food, and getting it all on the table, along with the plates and knives and forks and the big Mason jars we drank tea from, was going to take a while. But Grandma had stopped moving. She stood there next to the sink, listening, and so did I.

"I can't sleep in this bed," Nick said. "I can't shit in that toilet, I can't eat at that table. Hell, I'd be scared of the food."

We couldn't hear what Lynn said, but in some form or fashion she must have asked him why.

"Because," he said, "I haven't ever done it before."

I did not, at that time, understand that a fair amount of what is wrong with the world on any particular day, in any particular century, is apt to be the result of somebody's

unwillingness to experience something he's never experienced before. I did not, at that time, even understand what a person like Nick would find wrong with the bed I'd so often slept in or the toilet I'd relieved myself in almost every day of my life.

But there was one thing I knew for sure: If he sat down at Grandma's table and ate this meal, he might very well want to spend the remainder of his life in this house.

Of that there could be no doubt.

Many years later, after I moved to California to teach at a university, my cousin Lynn came to visit my wife and my daughters and me. She still lived in Texarkana but she and Nick had been divorced for almost ten years. She was in her mid-fifties, a tall silver-haired woman with a deeply tanned face. She came to Fresno in a new Mercedes. It was one of the V-12s, a car that cost more than our house.

She said the Mercedes belonged to the man she was seeing. He lived in Orange County. He was a developer, she said. She'd met him the previous summer on the beach in Key West.

In the backyard, while I cooked burgers on my gas grill, I asked her if things between her and the developer were serious.

"When you're my age," she said, "everything's serious."

She had called me a few days earlier and said she was on the West Coast and would like to visit. She had read

both my books, she said, and she was proud to have an author in the family.

"And you're a college professor, too," she said. "That's wonderful."

I believed she meant it, but as I stood there flipping burgers, it crossed my mind that maybe she'd learned her lesson. Our English Tudor might have looked as lowly to her Orange County magnate as Grandma's house had looked to Nick. Maybe that's why she'd come to see us by herself.

At dinner that night she asked my daughters lots of questions about their school and their hobbies, and she asked my wife, Eva, who is Polish, lots of questions about Poland. Lynn said she and the developer had talked about visiting Eastern Europe next spring. They were mostly interested in seeing Prague and Budapest, but she said they might put Kraków on their list, too.

Then she leaned back, surveyed the four of us, and said, "It's nice to see two people from such different backgrounds make such a wonderful family."

That seemed as good a time as any to raise the specter of Nick. Where was he now, I asked her; what was he doing?

She said he managed a factory in Bryan, Texas. She never saw him anymore, and neither did her sons. The last few years they were all together, she said, had been pretty awful.

"But you know what?" she said, brightening. "He never did quit talking about that meal your grandma cooked him. You remember that night we stayed there?"

I said I did.

"He always wanted me to cook catfish that way and hush puppies, too, but I never could do it to satisfy him. He said that meal your grandma cooked him was the best he ever ate in his life."

"Do you remember the pictures?" I asked.

"What pictures?"

"The ones Grandma sent you after y'all had been to see us."

Lynn frowned. "I'd forgotten those," she said. "Hey, what was that all about anyway?"

All of us sat at the table in the dining room. Nick and Lynn, Mother and Dad and I, Grandma and Grandpa. Nick was accorded a place of honor at the end of the table.

He had changed clothes. He was wearing white pants and a short-sleeved Hawaiian shirt. It looked like he'd rubbed another layer of Brylcreem on his hair. It was stiff now and shiny.

He sat there with his arms crossed, staring at his plate, steeling himself for the worst. *The Beverly Hillbillies* had entered the American consciousness the year before, and you could tell he was preparing himself for the kinds of

concoctions Granny Clampitt might serve. Possum fried in lard, owl cutlets, stewed groundhog—that sort of thing.

Earlier, when Grandma and I were still in the kitchen and they were in the bedroom, Grandma and I had heard Lynn pleading with him. "She's my favorite aunt. She helped Momma raise me. Please, just bear it tonight, and we'll leave in the morning. They can't help it if they're poor."

"I knew they were poor," we heard him say. "I was ready for that. It's unsanitary here. That's what worries me. Who know whether or not the food's safe to eat?"

"It's safe. They've been eating it all their lives. I used to eat it, too."

"If I get sick," he grumbled, "you better haul me to a hospital quick."

Now, the catfish and the hush puppies had been dumped onto a huge green platter, which rested in the middle of the table. The coleslaw was in a big brown bowl. A bottle of Hunt's ketchup stood near the catfish. The plates that we would eat from were three different varieties. There were four heavy brown plates, a couple of white plates with Christmas designs around the rims, and one off-white plate that had no design at all on it, though if you turned it upside down you would find an inscription on the bottom. The inscription read: PROPERTY OF SOUTH SUNFLOWER COUNTY HOSPITAL.

"Nick," Grandpa said, "you want to say grace?"

It was customary to ask the guest to say the blessing. No one had ever refused. But Nick Miller did. "I'm not the churchgoing type," he said.

"We got married in church," Lynn blurted out.

"Yeah, we did," Nick said. "But it was mostly just a social occasion."

For the last half-hour, ever since we'd overheard the argument between Nick and Lynn, Grandma had been silent. She had replied to every question I'd asked her about setting the table with a shake of her head. Now she said, "Ain't this a social occasion?"

As I've said, we didn't know much about Nick except that he played football in college. We also knew that he worked for some company of sorts, that he was an executive, a man who wore a suit to work and gave orders and fired people. He didn't own the company, though, so he must have taken orders, too. He must, at some time, have found himself in a position in which his word was questioned. Knowing what I know now about people like Nick Miller, I will risk a guess and say that when his word was questioned by a superior, he behaved in a very obliging, perhaps apologetic manner.

But Grandma was not his superior. He uncrossed his arms, laid his arms down flat on the table, and spread his fingers out as if he were getting ready for action.

"Well, now," he said, "ain't this a social occasion? Yes, by doggie, it sure enough is."

While the rest of us sat there stunned, Nick Miller bowed his head and shut his eyes. "Jesus," he said, doing his best to sound like Billy Graham. "Yes, *Jeez Us*. Bless these fish. Bless these hush puppies. Bless this house and them that's in it. Bless the dogs and the cows and the chickens and the pigs. Bless all their leavings in the yard outside. Bless the hay and the cotton and the soybeans and John Deere. Bless this cole, coleslaw as you bless our hard, hard hearts."

And then Nick Miller raised his head and opened his eyes and picked up his fork. "Let's eat," he said.

He stabbed a piece of fish and laid it on his plate, then he picked up a hush puppy and popped it in his mouth, and when he started to chew, I swear you could see a light enter his eyes. Slowly, while he and he alone ate, while the rest of us sat there and watched as he swallowed one hush puppy after another, as he ate piece after piece of catfish, and pile upon pile of coleslaw, as stains appeared on his Hawaiian shirt, and his hands became so greasy he wiped them on his thighs, the snobbery drained out of his face.

I didn't know that day what it was that had left him, and I didn't know that it would leave for only a little while and then come surging back, but I knew in my heart that his heart had softened. And I knew what had brought on

the change: not the prayer he had spoken, but the meal he had eaten.

At Grandma's table, the food was a blessing in itself.

But having said that, I am saddened to have to say this.

Just as the blessing wore off Nick Miller, so that a few years down the road, after *Deliverance* hit the screens, he would disrupt cocktail parties by suggesting certain familial links between Lynn and the mountain men who raped Ned Beatty, the blessing wore off the food on Grandma's table.

The change, unlike the change that had overcome Nick that night in 1963, was not sudden. It came about gradually. It came with many other changes that, at first glance, would seem to have little or nothing to do with food. Grandma began to look at new cars. You would sometimes see her walking around the lot at the Pontiac dealership or, at other times, down the road at the Ford dealership. Finally, she found the one she wanted, a new cream-colored Tempest. I remember the day she drove it home. She parked it in the front yard, near the chinaberry tree, in almost exactly the same spot where Nick Miller had parked his silver Cadillac. Grandpa's pickup truck had never looked strange there, but the Tempest, so shiny and new, seemed out of place. And so, a few years later, Grandma told Grandpa she wanted him to build a carport.

She bought a new refrigerator with an ice maker in it, and she bought a color TV. She visited Lott's Furniture Company and bought linoleum rugs for each room in the house. She bought a stereo, though she almost never turned it on, and she bought several standing lamps and a new bathtub and toilet. She repapered the walls in every room.

She quit raising chickens. When Grandpa's dog Buster showed the first signs of illness, she insisted Grandpa shoot him, and they never had a dog again. She made Grandpa nail tin siding around the bottom of the house so that animals could not get under it.

She began to buy canned or frozen vegetables, and these were what we ate for supper. She discovered Swanson frozen roast beef and gravy. It came in a pouch, and all you had to do was drop the pouch in boiling water for three or four minutes, and you had yourself a main dish. She bought apple pies frozen. She bought pecan pies that came in a box with a clear layer of plastic on top, so you could see the pie, which had been baked in Cincinnati or St. Louis within the last two weeks. She developed a preference for Wonder bread. Any suggestion that it was made of Styrofoam would turn her livid. "I've got better things to do," she would say, "than stand in the kitchen half the day making pies and corn bread. This ain't the days of covered wagons. This is the modern world, and I for one refuse to regret it."

One night, two or three years after Nick and Lynn came to visit, she brought a Polaroid camera into the dining room where Grandpa and I sat, resigned to a supper of Oscar Mayer weenies chopped into links and buried in a casserole dish full of Kraft macaroni and cheese. Alongside that, on one of Grandma's new plates from the set of chinaware she'd bought at United Dollar Store, was half a loaf of Wonder bread, all the slices stacked neatly on top of one another. A blueberry pie, still in the box, was next to the bread.

"What are you doing?" Grandpa said.

He thought she planned to take a picture of him and me. I thought so, too. But when she aimed the camera, she aimed at the food. The flash clicked once, then twice, and she was gone.

Afterword

Companions are those with whom we share bread. The word is derived from Latin, *com*, "together," and *panis*, "bread." By sharing their memories and stories of food, the eloquent contributors to this book have proven themselves companions in the fight against hunger, in the truest sense of the word. All of us at Share Our Strength are grateful for their gifts. As the founder and director of Share Our Strength for the past fifteen years, I've seen the impact that results from powerful voices and new resources.

Once when I was very young, in the cool, damp basement of the house where my sister and I grew up in Pittsburgh, my best friend and I tried to build an airplane. Not

a model airplane, but a real one! It was an ambitious un-
dertaking and we both sunk all of our allowances into
it. Then, as now, airplane parts were quite expensive. So,
in addition to the fact that we knew nothing about build-
ing airplanes, early on we faced the classic dilemma: we
couldn't buy the tools and materials we needed, so instead
we bought the tools and materials we could afford. The
airplane never flew.

The national network of organizations fighting
hunger in America, unfortunately, are forced to approach
their task in much the same way. Without more support,
they are destined to suffer the same result.

Available funds are so inadequate against the magni-
tude of the hunger problem that most well-meaning orga-
nizations focus on whatever strategies they can afford,
rather than the strategies most needed to end hunger. As
a result, dollar after dollar is spent on larger and more ef-
ficient food banks, canned food drives, soup kitchens,
community gardens, and other measures that relieve
hunger, but woefully little is targeted at the root cause of
hunger which is poverty.

Without substantially more resources devoted to com-
munity development, economic opportunity, advocacy,
job training and readiness, and education, the effort to
truly abolish hunger in America simply won't get off the
ground.

Share Our Strength is determined to change this. Our unique and comprehensive grant-making strategy funds all of the above. It is based on the understanding that it takes more than food to fight hunger.

Hard times test our generosity and character as a people and a nation. But so too, in a different way, do good times. These are indeed good times, and our blessings are not to be denied. The economy is strong and America is at peace. Yet more Americans are seeking food assistance than ever before.

These are the conditions under which we can and should mount a successful campaign to eliminate hunger in America once and for all. This book is part of that campaign. And now you are too.

William H. Shore
Executive Director
Share Our Strength

LIST OF CONTRIBUTORS

Julia Alvarez is a poet, fiction writer and essayist. Her latest novel is *Yo!*. A new book of essays, *Something to Declare*, will be published in 1999. Julia Alvarez lives in Vermont.

Paul Auster's novels include *The New York Trilogy (City of Glass, Ghosts, The Locked Room), In the Country of Last Things, Moon Palace, The Music of Chance, Leviathan*, and *Mr. Vertigo*. He is also the author of a memoir, *The Invention of Solitude*, and a collection of essays, *The Art of Hunger*. His last book was *Hand to Mouth*. He lives in Brooklyn with his wife and two children.

Charles Baxter is the author of four collections of stories, most recently *Believers*, published by Pantheon, and two novels, *First Light* and *Shadow Play*, available in paperback from Penguin. He also wrote a book of essays on fiction, *Burning Down the House*, published by Graywolf Press. He teaches at the University of Michigan and lives in Ann Arbor.

Madison Smartt Bell is the Director of the Creative Writing Program at Goucher College. He is the author of a handful of novels, most recently *Ten Indians* and *All Souls Rising*. He's currently at work on a nonfiction book about contemporary Haiti as well as the second volume of a trilogy on the Haitian slave revolution. He lives in Baltimore with his wife, the poet Elizabeth Spires.

Wendell Berry taught at colleges in New York and California before returning to his native Kentucky where he writes and farms 125 acres in Henry County.

Janet Burroway is the author of plays, poetry, essays, children's books, and seven novels including *The Buzzards*, *Raw Silk*, *Opening Nights*, and *Cutting Stone*. She writes a regular column for *New Letters* magazine, and reviews frequently for the *New York Times Book Review*. Her text, *Writing Fiction*, now in its fourth printing, is used in more

than 300 colleges and universities in the U.S. She is Robert O. Lawton Distinguished Professor of English at Florida State University.

Elena Castedo's fiction, essays, poetry, and a play, in English and Spanish, have won numerous awards. *Paradise*, published in several countries, is the first novel to win nominations or major prizes in the author's English and Spanish versions, including a nomination for the 1990 National Book Award and Chile's *El Mercurio* "Book of the Year" award. She lectures, teaches seminars, and writes for the Spanish press.

John Dufresne's work has appeared in numerous journals, including the *Mississippi Review*, *Missouri Review*, and the *Greensboro Review*. He is the author of the novels *Louisiana Power & Light* and *Love Warps the Mind a Little*, as well as the short story collection, *The Way That Water Enters Stone*. He lives in South Florida with his wife and son.

Robert Girardi is the author of three novels, *Madeleine's Ghost*, *The Pirate's Daughter*, and *Vaporetto 13*, all published by Delacorte. He lives in Washington, D.C., with his wife and daughter.

Jessica B. Harris, a professor at Queens College CUNY, is a food historian and the author of seven cookbooks, the

most recent of which is *Africa: A Continent of Cuisine*. She lives in New York.

David Haynes is the author of *All American Dream Dolls, Live at Five*, and *Somebody Else's Mama*.

Gish Jen is the author of *Typical American* and *Mona in the Promised Land*.

Beverly Lowry has written essays and feature articles for many magazines. She is the author of six novels, the most recent of which is *The Track of Real Desires*. She is also the author of a book of nonfiction, *Crossed Over*, about Carla Faye Tucker.

Bobbie Ann Mason is the bestselling author of *In Country, Spence + Lila*, and *Shiloh and Other Stories*. She lives in Lawrenceburg, Kentucky.

Jill McCorkle was born and raised in Lumberton, North Carolina. She graduated from the University of North Carolina at Chapel Hill and received an M.F.A. in Creative Writing from Hollins College. She has written five novels, the most recent of which is *Carolina Moon*. Her latest short story collection is *Final Vinyl Days*. She teaches in the Bennington College MFA Program and lives in the Boston area with her husband and two children.

Gita Mehta is the author of three novels, *Karma Cola*, *Raj*, and *A River Sutra*, as well as *Snakes and Ladders*, a collection of essays. Her work has appeared in many Indian, American, and European magazines and has been translated into 13 languages in 27 countries. She has filmed documentaries for both European and American television. She lives in New York, London, and India.

Ellen Meloy, possibly the only weaned American who has never in her entire life eaten at McDonald's, writes from her home in southern Utah. She is the author of two natural histories, *Raven's Exile: A Season on the Green River* and *The Last Cheater's Waltz*, both from Holt. In 1997 the Whiting Foundation honored her with a Writer's Award.

Lorrie Moore is a professor of English at the University of Wisconsin and lives in Madison. Her work has appeared in *The New Yorker, The Best American Short Stories*, and *Prize Stories: The O. Henry Awards*. She is the author of three collections of stories, *Self-Help*, *Like Life*, and, most recently, *Birds of America*, and the novels *Anagrams* and *Who Will Run the Frog Hospital?*

Josip Novakovich was born in Croatia in 1956 and has lived in the USA since 1976. He is the author of an essay collection, *Apricots from Chernobyl*, and two collections of stories, *Yoke* and *Salvation and Other Disasters*. He has won